Daisy Buchanan is an award-winning journalist, the host of the iTunes Number One podcast, *You're Booked*, and the author of the critically acclaimed book *How To Be A Grown Up*. She's a regular contributor to TV and radio, frequently appearing on *Woman's Hour*, *Good Morning Britain*, *This Morning*, *Sky News* and the Today programme. Daisy writes for a wide range of publications including the *Guardian*, *The Telegraph*, *The Times*, *The Sun*, *Grazia*, *Marie Claire* and *The Pool*, covering everything from pop culture to mental health with a feminist perspective. She's a TEDx speaker, giving advice on how to get through the trickiest parts of your twenties in her talk *How To Survive A Quarter Life Crisis*. Daisy has been *Grazia's* in house agony aunt, writing the popular 'Dear Daisy' column, and she's currently the title's Reality TV correspondent, covering *Made In Chelsea* with her tongue firmly in her cheek.

Also by Daisy Buchanan and available from Headline

How to Be a Grown-Up

the
sisterhood

a love letter to the women who have shaped us

daisy buchanan

HEADLINE

For the women I love, and the women they love.

First published in 2019 by
HEADLINE PUBLISHING GROUP

First published in paperback in 2020 by
HEADLINE PUBLISHING GROUP

1

Cataloguing in Publication Data is available from the British Library

ISBN 978 1 4722 3886 3

Typeset in Adobe Garamond Pro
by Palimpsest Book Production Ltd, Falkirk, Stirlingshire

Printed and bound in Great Britain by Clays Ltd, Elcograf S.p.A.

Headline's policy is to use papers that are natural, renewable and recyclable
products and made from wood grown in well-managed forests and other controlled
sources. The logging and manufacturing processes are expected to conform to
the environmental regulations of the country of origin.

HEADLINE PUBLISHING GROUP
An Hachette UK Company
Carmelite House
50 Victoria Embankment
London
EC4Y 0DZ

www.headline.co.uk
www.hachette.co.uk

Contents

Introduction   1

1. Being the Biggest   9

2. Bodies and Appetites   22
   A Room of One's Own   35

3. The House of Puberty   39

4. Once a Catholic   53
   Beth   66

5. How Do I Look? Like You!   69

6. Too Many Feelings   74

7. King Lear, Cinderella and Me   86
   The Best Books About Sisters   96

8. The Christmas Chapter   99
   The Fairy Dress   104

9. Fierce, Fraught and Fabulous: 107
   Grace   124

10. Womanhood and Girl-on-Girl Judgement   128

11. Millennial Women and the Anxiety Epidemic   135
    Liv   145

12. Family Car Journeys, a Love Letter   149
     August 2011: The Band Gets Back Together   155

13. Surrogate Sisters and Women at Work   158
     Lauren   164

14. Comedy and Drama   170
     Maddy   182

15. Is It Bad to Be Bossy?   186

16. Are You Suffering from Big Sister Syndrome?   195
     Dotty   205

17. Sisters in Love and Law   209

18. How to Be a Grown-up Sister   224

19. Death and the Maidens   240

20. My Advice for My Sisters   250
     The Worst Things to Say to Sisters   259

Conclusion: What Is Sisterhood?   261

Acknowledgements   265

Introduction

My five sisters are the only women I'd kill for. And they're the only women I sometimes want to kill. My experience of sisterhood is to be in a perpetual state of fury, adoration and near hysteria. These women are wicked, and pure. These women make my guts feel like fire and treacle. I have cried over them a thousand times, and laughed to a point that felt meditative – hot wet salt coursing down my cheeks, fist striking my thigh, as I try to explain myself ('It's just . . . it's just when she . . . I can't . . . HO! Arghhhhhhhh!'). We understand each other in a way we can't understand ourselves.

But they're not my best friends. We constantly keep secrets from each other, discovering them six months later. Stories of bad sex, credit card debt, crying in the night, hospital appointments – we protect each other from so many horror stories, and I'm not sure it's wholly healthy. We throw our hands up like fishermen, talking about The Anecdote That Got Away. 'It's funny now! But I nearly died! Didn't I tell you?' No, no, no.

We're all built to the same vague specification. Thick hair, thick legs, narrow waists and low voices. When more than one of us is laughing, it sounds like a scene in a bad mob movie

1

where one person gets a machine gun out of a violin case and there's a sudden rat-a-tat-tat cacophony of bullets. Our voices are almost identical, and we sound like exactly the same person adapting to six different scenarios. I sound like an actress talking on the telephone in an imaginary BBC radio play called *Stiff Upper Lip, Chaps*. Beth talks as though she's been caught by surprise with a visit from the plumber. Grace sounds like a Head Girl presenting prizes on sports day; Liv as if she's doing an impression of Russell Brand doing an impression of someone from Somerset; Maddy is all of the above, in treble; and Dotty has a surprise deep bass boom at the end. It causes much confusion when the phone rings. A little while ago, Grace phoned our parents, and Beth picked it up, and the two of them spoke to each other for twenty minutes before realising that each thought the other was speaking to Liv.

Still, on some days, we don't seem the same at all. There are countless variations, sometimes within the same sister. I am always shocked by how alike, and how *unlike* we all are. It's dangerously easy for me to assume that I know what they're thinking and feeling, and that we understand each other completely. As children, we wasted weeks of our summer holidays attempting to prove our telepathy. I'd push my forehead against Beth's, believing I could extract the secrets of her mind by osmosis and brute force. 'The number you're thinking of is sev-nine . . . WENTY!' Or we'd climb into cupboards and try to will the sister on the other side of the door to intercept secret messages, a game that quickly lost all psychic magic and devolved into repeatedly whispering the word 'poohead'.

But my baby sisters have grown into independent women,

and the only way for me to find out how they are, and who they are, is to ask. We are not six parts of a whole. We don't always fit together well. As adults, we've found the space to explore the fact that we have identities beyond 'sister'. When sisterhood feels like a choice, we can cherish it.

But what does sisterhood mean? Is it a fixed state? Is it an integral part of feminism, or does it hold us back by forcing us to feel as though we're not good women unless we're constantly being nice to each other?

In my parents' house, in the downstairs loo, on a scalloped shelf that kept falling off the wall, and has now been repurposed as a book case, there are several books about sisters. They have names like *In Praise of Sisterhood* and *The Bliss of Sisterhood*. The covers are always decorated with Pre-Raphaelite paintings of peaceful women who have long, cloudy dark hair and enormous nipples. I don't know why. Possibly, it's because most of these images are now out of copyright, and cheap to use. Maybe it's because even the most high-minded members of society can't bring themselves to think of women spending time together unless they're being nearly naked and slightly sexy. Even though I am almost never plaiting my sisters' long, straight hair, while lying on a lawn and contemplating their nipples. More than one man has found out that I have five sisters and *immediately* asked, 'So, did you ever . . . practise kissing, with each other?' (There is only one answer to this: 'Well, did you and your brothers practise hand jobs with each other?') These tit-ular siblings imply sisterhood is sleepy, and sexual. Sisters are meant to be calm, and maybe to fancy each other a bit. For vanity's sake, if nothing else. After all, we all look alike.

Sisters are the prism through which female connectedness has been explored and understood by many writers. I grew up with the March girls and the Bennet sisters, then found myself keeping company with the Kardashians. Why are we so interested in sisters? One of the most famous women in the world – Kim, who is, like the fictional Elizabeth Bennet, the second born and the narrative star – became a celebrity in the context of sisterhood. Her sisters are almost as famous as she is, and they all star in one of the longest-running reality programmes in US history. Millions of viewers turn in because they want to know what it's like to be a sister, or maybe how the Kardashian experience of sisterhood is similar and different from their own. Maybe they're like me, and they want reassurance that it's OK to love your sisters and occasionally hate them at the same time. That the most beautiful women in the world still cry ugly tears and sometimes say ugly things to the people they adore the most.

Sisters in books are kind, patient and wise – or they're punished for their failure to be so. The canon says that the good sister may marry a good man, and the jealous sister will have sex out of wedlock and be drowned in a well, and the village will come together to sing a song about her lack of moral fibre. However, the most vivid depiction I have ever seen of a relationship that's anything like the one I have with my sisters is this: a sketch on a long-forgotten comedy programme called *Beehive*, in which one woman, dressed as Tom Cruise, tried to wrangle another gang of women, dressed as priests, into a minivan. It's obscure, but it's the metaphor that best fits the strange, hilarious, ongoing drama of sisterhood.

Introduction

At any given time, half of us will be shouting and the other half will be laughing at them. This is partly because we don't feel the need to be especially feminine around each other. We're as relaxed as drunken priests on a parish outing, and as aggressively confident as award-winning actors who think it's OK to jump on Oprah's furniture. We speak without fear of censure, and the only rule is: be funny or die. Normally, being a woman is like being a Catholic, in that we're required to spend every waking hour resisting all of our natural impulses. We're all both Catholic and female, yet when we're together we find blissful release from this pressure, simply because we can sit with our legs apart and fart freely.

When I'm out in the world I become very anxious about how I'm perceived. It seems important that I come across as a girl and a woman, and I perform femininity as a reflex, because I'm frightened that I will be shamed for not being feminine enough. (I'm delighted that we live in an era of non-binary gender fluidity but I will never recover from the autumn of 1995, when everyone in the playground became very aerated about the fact that I was wearing boys' shoes because my feet were so big.) For me, the solace of sisterhood is finding a space where we can stop performing. We don't need to try to be cute, or girly or delicate. It doesn't matter whether a sister is biological or simply logical, she's a person who makes you feel like the woman you are, not the woman you feel you should pretend to be. While we'll always hold back parts of ourselves and share others by degrees, I know that when I'm with my sisters I'm not the best version of myself, but the truest.

Our family photos prove this. The less flattering the

image, the more honest it is. We have pictures taken at weddings and twenty-first birthdays where, for less than half a second, we have all managed to smile sweetly and look in the same direction. None of these photos really look like us. The only one that comes close is a souvenir photo from Thorpe Park. We're on the rapids. The shutter went down at a point when I was half way through my smile, and I had just started to wonder about the quality of water that had entered my mouth. Grace has her head in her hands, because she's convinced the camera lens is going to squirt her. Olivia is patting a pocket, looking for her phone or her cigarettes, because riding a giant tire on a fake lake while enduring regular drenchings is the *perfect* time for a fag. Maddy is cowering, also because of the water. Dotty is enjoying Maddy's cowering even more than she is enjoying the ride itself. And Beth is not there, because during this period of her life, she has a great disdain for group activities *and* theme parks. This disdain will dissipate six months after this picture is taken, when she moves to Blackpool and gets a season ticket for the Pleasure Beach. I think that's the biggest, hardest part of being part of a big group of sisters. You can't always run in a pack. Someone is always excluded, either accidentally or on purpose.

One of the worst things about being a woman is that you're constantly being asked why you're not more like a different woman or told that you should be doing your best to imitate another woman altogether. It's worse when you're a sister, because you're always being made to feel like a failure for not being Amal Clooney, Mother Teresa *and* the person who is sitting opposite you and has scored the ultimate life goal – finishing their peas. 'Why are your sisters so different?'

people ask. I can only assume that they skipped every single biology class on their timetable to go and smoke at the bottom of a football pitch. (My mother, the comic genius, once met the standard line about our inconsistencies with: 'Well, they all have different fathers!' *Especially* ballsy given she was at a parents' evening.)

For a long time, I had an unfair advantage. As the eldest sister, I set the tone. Beth's shyness was unfairly contrasted with my 'have-a-go hero' sensibility. Grace's scientific aptitude was met with as much suspicion as if she had expressed a predilection for sorcery – yet, if she had turned up first, I would be disappointing science teachers all over the south east. Olivia, Madeleine and Dorothy are now adult women with exciting lives and careers, but for years, their actions were predicted and pre-empted because of the girls we were before. It wasn't fair. It isn't fair. We have been judged as sisters, and now we are judged as women. We're told we're atypical, when there is no typical – just a narrow idea that someone else came up with a long, long time ago.

Even when I've *hated* my sisters and spent afternoons hitting them with an old roll of wallpaper I found in a cupboard under the stairs, I have never doubted their intellectual powers. (I've questioned my own, especially as I screamed, 'DIE! DIE FROM HAUNTED WALLPAPER!' My parents bought their house from the widow of a solicitor who lived peacefully and died of old age, in his sleep. I'm confident that his spirit had no unfinished business that concerned interior decoration.) When you grow up with a gang of girls, you build your own matriarchy. You're not defining yourself in opposition to boys and men. Your sense

of your own femininity becomes a fact of your existence
rather than a tool you need to employ for your own defence.
It never crosses your mind that cleverness and funniness aren't
female traits, because you're with clever, funny women all day
long. We can help ourselves and each other become stronger
and more powerful if we come together to understand what
we're up against – and then laugh about it.

Sisterhood is *hard*. When we're with our sisters, we can
feel jealous, insecure, undermined and controlling. Sometimes
we feel left out and alone. We see reflected sides of ourselves
that we can't bear. Yet, I believe that embracing sisterhood is
about finding peace among women. You can love some with
your heart, while being annoyed and infuriated with the
others as long as you remember that you're playing for a team.
It's OK to strike out as an individual as long as you're
promoting the interests of the team too, because if you hold
them back, you're going to be holding yourself back in the
long run. You can all believe in different things, as long as
you believe in each other.

CHAPTER ONE
Being the Biggest

I am the eldest child. The first daughter. The best, the most, the one who must constantly run out in front, run as though her life depends on it – even though she has the athletic ability of an asthmatic cabbage. I set a standard for myself, simply by being born, and I fall short of that standard every day that I fail to win an Oscar or broker a peace treaty.

All of my earliest memories have the word 'sister' in them. I was born in the spring of 1985, when my mother was twenty-five, and my father was twenty-seven. Beth was born in the summer of 1986, and so I don't remember a world without her. I do remember being threatened and cajoled into being nice to her. 'Don't hit Beth!' 'Why don't you give Beth a hug?' 'Give your sweeties to Beth!' 'Stop hitting Beth with that plastic truck!' It's only now that I think about how difficult it must have been for my parents to look after two tiny girls before either of them turned thirty. I had no sense of my own tininess – Beth's very existence made me 'big', even though I was three to her two.

The first time I heard the playground rhyme 'First the worst, second the best', I responded as though it were a personal attack. Being first was at the very core of my being. It was all I had, and I could not be chill about it. My parents were constantly trying to explain that the eldest child had a great responsibility, to set a good example, to be kind and clever, a decent role model that my sisters could look up to. The trouble with this is that I assumed that if I had all this responsibility, I must have Great Power too. What was the point of all this constant goodness if I couldn't abuse my position?

Admittedly I lacked the imagination to contrive any abuses of power that were not sweet-based. As more sisters arrived and the opportunities for sibling-based domination grew, my fiendish plans were usually executed in this way:

1. Setting up a club. I'd gather my Winnie the Pooh clipboard and parade enticingly around the house, tapping my nose with a Bic Biro, before getting exasperated, hurling it to the ground, approaching various sisters and saying, 'Do you want to be in my club?' and then 'Mum says you have to be in my club,' then 'Be in my club or I'll bite you.'

2. Telling sisters that they had to attend our 'first meeting', which could take place in any room as long as I had purloined a piece of printer paper, stuck it to the door and written 'HEADQUARTERS' on it. (OK, let's be real, I often wrote 'HEADQUATERS'.)

3. Telling sisters that they had to bring any sweets they had. I had heard the expression 'refreshments will be provided' and I believed it could be used as a dark threat. 'Refreshments will be provided. By you. Or else.'

4. Making everyone sit on the floor, while I sat on a bed or chair. There would be a tussle while I forced

someone, probably Beth or Grace to take the 'minutes' (where did I learn about taking minutes?), before grabbing the pad from them and saying, 'No, I have won a PRIZE FOR HANDWRITING, your writing is not good enough for the club.'

5. Demanding that every club member handed over their sweets, to be kept in a drawer, which I would monitor as president and treasurer. Over the next day, I would eat every single sweet before disbanding the club.

Looking back, I'm very surprised that I have not gone into business, or at least attempted the Alec Baldwin role in a local amateur production of *Glengarry Glen Ross*. I had very clear objectives – early onset diabetes – and I would do whatever it took to meet those objectives, including bullying, manipulating and lying to the people who were the closest to me. At the time, I thought it was all about amassing a vast cache of Chewits and Jelly Tots, but now I realise that my poor sisters were victims of my appalling status anxiety. I had to boss them about because I believed nature had made me the boss. I felt I was born to rule, like James I, albeit with a superior collection of felt-tip pens. Yet I wasn't enjoying any part of the performance, especially not the Technicolored vomit.

Even without my Bolshevik tendencies and sweetie requisitioning, I was a difficult big sister. It didn't help that I was a hard act to follow. I think Beth suffered the purest agonies of comparison, being sixteen months younger than me, and directly behind me. Every single one of us was academically gifted, but Beth was gloriously weird. For a while, my smug status was cast in bronze because our teachers longed for her to be more like her big, boring sister, and less prone to writing strange, vivid dream essays, or collecting snails in an old Gino Ginelli tub. Being the eldest cemented my legend, and every time someone asked a sibling why they couldn't be more like their sister, they were painting a picture of a Me who was Not Me, a Daisy who was steady and slow, diligent and willing. I didn't always feel like the sister that the teachers referred to, but apparently she was I. Every time one of the others was told off or punished for not being good enough, I felt as though I had been praised for setting the bar unreachably high.

It might not surprise you to know that this is a toxic way to raise children. Also, it meant that every time my sisters did well, I felt as though I was being punched in the face and mugged. I still remember Beth phoning from school with her GCSE results. I did not exclaim, 'Well done! Has a pervy local photographer turned up to take a picture of you leaping up into the air?' I think I said, 'That's one more fucking A-star than I got, YOU BITCH!' and slammed the phone down. At that moment, it felt as though Beth had found the drawer where my own certificates were kept and burned them. As though she might have spent extra hours working and revising purely to beat me and make me feel bad. That she might have a picture of my face on her History folder, with a big red Sharpie cross through my face, as hate-spiration.

Half my lifetime later, I am just about able to say, 'Well done, Beth! Those were excellent and deserved GCSE results!' This has taken sixteen years, and at least three of those years have been spent in therapy.

I think the worst thing about being the eldest sister is that no one else cares or congratulates you for being born first. It's a status quo that comes dangerously close to defining you and every relationship you have. But it is never useful or helpful. I can't email an editor of a newspaper and say, 'I'm the eldest, and I suspect some of the people you employ might be younger children, so you should let me be in charge and give me a column, as well as any Smarties you might have on you.' To the best of my knowledge, even the maddest and most arrogant Tinder bios do not say, 'I am the eldest one in my family so you must swipe right, take me out for a steak the size of a toilet seat and a lobster champagne smoothie, and then immediately propose marriage.' It's not as if I've ever even enjoyed the sense of being first. It's more that I've felt utterly miserable when I'm not, as if I've failed at the one thing I was born to do.

Of course, it's difficult for every single one of my sisters too. I'd like to believe that Beth's originality and creativity is a two-fingered salute to anyone who ever told her that she wasn't similar enough to me, but I look back and feel furious about everyone who told her to be less proudly strange – that they'd prefer her if she were quieter, smaller and easier to manage. Recently I was talking to Grace, who spent her time at school as an academic superstar who excelled at absolutely everything – even Textiles. (She is the only sister whose Year Eight cushion project was not hastily finished by Mum, over the Easter holidays.) 'I was just trying to impress you, and catch up,' she says. 'I only ever wanted to be as good as you, and it was exhausting!' This was news to me. I used to think that Grace was woken up by someone throwing medals and certificates at her, and she wouldn't get out of bed for less than 10,000 awards.

Only one person can be first, and it's not the same person every time. It's really difficult to cheer and applaud when someone else passes the line before you, when you have all been running towards the same thing. I think that's one of the toughest things about having siblings that are extremely close in age. When you're growing up together, you're all pitching in the same general direction. When you're all women, I think it's harder still. You don't see that many women succeeding, being exciting, getting rewarded for their hard work and becoming the centre of attention. According to the movies, if you're extremely lucky and special, you might get to be the beautiful partner of a successful man, or her sassy friend.

One of the biggest arguments I ever had with Beth was about a late eighties cartoon called *Vicky the Viking*. Beth was adamant that Vicky was a boy. I was convinced that Vicky must be a girl, because she had a girl's name and long blonde hair. So convinced that I took all of the cushions off the sofa, then forced Beth to lie on the springy seat, before reinstating the cushions and sitting on her. In the eighties, cartoons were currency. I wanted an animated female role model so badly that I was prepared to engage in an act of violence against women to have one. (It's worth pointing out that the second biggest argument I had with Beth was about who could pretend to be Rosey, the heroine of Rosanne Barr's early nineties cartoon show, *Little Rosey.* No one got to be Rosey because we were both sent to bed for biting.)

Obviously, part of the transition from childhood to

adulthood involves learning that you can't hit people until they agree with you, and hand over the thing they have, because you've decided you want it. Still, I want to believe my heinous behaviour had another layer. When you see a woman or girl claiming space, existing in it freely, being confident and happy and receiving a manageable level of attention – about as much as Clare Balding, when she presents Crufts, and slightly less than Britney Spears in 2007 – you see a small, well-defined space that you can think about slotting into. And yet, you know how the world works well enough to realise that there's only space for a single person.

In the public eye, gangs of girls rarely fare well. If you're on a TV show with an ensemble cast, you must be best friends with your female colleagues, or you'll be castigated for being deadly enemies. If you want to make music with other women, other people will decide whether you're the hot one, the talented one, the fat one or the 'opinionated' one. (They'll come for you all, but the first one to be attacked will be the one who has something to say for herself. Anything at all is too much.) This is the trouble with being a sister. Everything you've ever heard seems to confirm that only one of you can be a star. Even Kelly Rowland could not claim to be the 'second lead singer' in her own family. You can resign yourself to singing back-up forever, or you can spend a lifetime scratching each other's faces and trying to flush each other's wigs down the loo.

We live in a world that is keen to encourage us all to be obsessed with winning. It's an insidious divide and conquer technique. Instead of collaborating and using our combined strength as an unstoppable superpower, it's much more convenient for everyone if we're played off against each other and spend all of our energy fighting each other instead of building each other up and creating new ideas and spaces. Our siblings stir any dormant feelings of competitiveness that we have. Even if we're naturally compassionate and curious about the people we're so close to, someone will suggest, often quite early on, that we should be making it our business to beat them.

Beth's early reaction to this – to celebrate the spirit of strangeness, and to strike out on her own as much as possible – might be the most sensible one. Even though she'd hate me for saying it. You can't compare weirdness, it's unique in its very nature. You can't be more or less weird than anyone else, simply strange in a different way. I found this infuriating. I couldn't win the competition if Beth insisted on playing a completely different game. Also, from a distance, we were considered to be exactly the same – perhaps not in personality, but certainly when it came to the distribution of stuff.

To be a sibling is to be forever estranged from contentment. Or, to put it another way, it's to find yourself crying into a pillow on the third day of the school German exchange, miserable and homesick, furious with yourself for going but even more furious about the idea that you could be at home, not experiencing the expensive school trip that all of your other sisters have 'enjoyed'. Have you ever been in an airport lounge and heard an angry man berating a busy waiter about the fact that someone else just ate the last chocolate cookie, and the replacement biscuits are an inferior pile of chewy garibaldis? I'd bet my all-you-can-drink prosecco allowance on that man having many brothers or sisters. We're constantly making calculations. Our fear of missing out is reinforced by a Fear of UnFairness, so my sisters and I share a FOUF. I get a pang in my FOUF every time I see that someone I follow on Instagram has been given a free T-shirt.

I believe this is an especially difficult era for my sisters and me, because our parents were so committed to making our lives as fair as possible. Even though we lived in the Conservative heartland of the Dorset countryside, our childhood had a Marxist quality, in which nothing was too small to be divided up into six separate bits. I think it shocked all of us when we grew up and realised that no one did this outside our family home. Other people thought we were insane if we were given a free Pret sandwich, and tried to divide it into nine tiny triangles, so it could be shared around the whole office. As a religious family, my sisters and I had an early introduction to the story of Jesus sharing bread and fish with thousands of people. We didn't think it was especially miraculous – not when Mum could make an entire family picnic with a Tuc cracker and a single pouch of Capri Sun.

In fact, our house had some of the qualities of a commune. When we moved from Buckinghamshire to Dorset in 1995, our parents battled property developers who believed that a slightly run down, three-floor Edwardian family house would make a great hotel, or retirement home. The house had belonged to a fabulously grand woman named Mrs Fitzroy, who had raised her own large family in it, over several decades, before age and ill health confined her to the ground floor. Privately I decided that I wanted to live there as soon as

I saw the chandelier in the space that the estate agents called the dining room, which was subsequently forever known as The Dining Room Not. (In the early nineties, the 'Not' joke had been incredibly popular, and my mother enjoyed using this joke domestically, and the sensation of feeling down with her kids. In 2006, *Borat* brought back the 'Not' joke and she was more surprised than anyone to find herself *au courant* with pop culture.)

For the last five years we had lived in a village in Buckinghamshire in a 'large, modern, five-bedroom detached house' – this is the way it was described in the *Daily Telegraph* when a fellow Brownie's mum interviewed my parents for a feature she was writing about large families. I think we had all been very unhappy in that house, what with my father and I being silently and sometimes violently bullied at work and school respectively, and infant Livvy nearly dying of a childhood illness. (We didn't know quite how ill she was until we were all a little older, so I'm going to be explaining it a little later.)   It was luxuriously equipped with pockets and corners for solitary, miserable dreaming. We had a cubbyhole, a large cupboard door built into the bedroom I once shared with Beth, that led to a space big enough to stand up in. There was a big garden with swings and a playhouse, a herb garden at the back of the property and a 'secret' garden, reached by running down a grassy slope on the left side of the house. We had a study with a piano, and a separate dining room (a luxury I suspect I will never know as an adult) which was overlooked by the drive, allowing our father to make a game of running out of the front door, holding our pudding and making a show of cooling our hot apple crumble and custard. Only now do I realise that my parents would have done anything within their power to make us laugh. That's love.

Yet, for a dreamy, pompous and precocious ten-year-old, the new house signified a thrilling new start. I'd read enough old books about old houses to convince myself that I was to the manor born, rather than to a bigger building moved. In this house, I could have my own room! The house had three floors, so for the first time in my life my sisters and I could hide from each other, unobserved. Even the presence of a fire extinguisher on the top floor landing made me proud. Our house was important! It was more flammable than the other houses!

The house was ambitious in design but there was a shabbiness in its bones, partly because of inevitable neglect and partly because it had been extended with great enthusiasm and ineptitude during the seventies. I like to think that everybody was simply too busy going to orgies and eating cocktail sausages to worry about boring things, like whether the door they had just built would fully fit the frame it was meant to rest in. The result was a sprawling building, for a sprawling family. We could go off on our own, or come together in dedicated spaces. We ate all of our meals in the breakfast room, we awaited the school run in the laundry room, and we were told off in the kitchen, part of the punishment being the claustrophobia induced by its narrowness and excessive brightness.

The house was built on a foundation of cognitive dissonance. It was large and luxurious enough to accommodate my individual delusions of grandeur, but chosen because it seemed to be the most suitable space available for a family that shared everything. It's difficult when you're raised as a sharer in a selfish, Western world, and harder still when, as a society, we're more collectively committed than ever before to the art of showing off. When I got my very first job* as a waitress and washer-upper at the Greyhound Pub in Corfe Castle, I awaited parental congratulations. Instead, the very first thing Dad said was, 'See if there's a job for Beth, too.' Yet, when someone shares news of a fabulous new job or promotion, they're taken aback when I ask if they can get me a similarly amazing opportunity, in the interests of fairness. Oddly, no one wants to split their new Audi six ways. When I really think about it, I don't want a sixth of an Audi. Or even a whole one. But the trouble with being part of a big family is that it can sometimes be difficult to understand what you genuinely want and need, and what you're distracted by, simply because someone else has it.

As an adult I've started to realise that I need to unlearn everything I thought I knew about fairness. I'm convinced that I'm constantly up against an army of under tens. I need to be hypervigilant about every single treat and award that everyone else gets, because I must have it too, otherwise it isn't *fair*. Even though the perpetual cry of parenthood seems to be 'Well, life isn't fair', I realise that my mum and dad put every single atom of their energy into making it as fair as

---

* If you ask my family, they may claim my first job was a paper round, which I managed half of, before Mum picked me up, and then finished the route the next day while I was at school. There is no proof that this ever happened, as the newsagent shut in 2006, still owing me £4.25.

possible for us. In a broader sense, of course, I've experienced countless advantages because of the unfairness of life. I have much, much more than most people, and it would be outrageous of me to not acknowledge this and do my best to redress the balance. However, to my shame, I still waste my time wanting what other people have, even though every day brings me more moments to be grateful for.

Now, I feel as though my sisters and I are a gang, a team and a unit – but when we were little, there were times when it seemed as though we were a disparate, bleeding, coal-smeared group of minor characters from the Mel Gibson-era *Mad Max* films. Every day was a war for more attention, more power and more biscuits. Survival depended on having just as much as everyone else, or more if possible, so that we could sustain ourselves on lean days. There is a reason why the *Mad Max* franchise has progressed and become a story of women working together to improve their prospects. Fairness can't flourish when everyone is out for themselves. Now I know that I don't need to fight to survive – it's better to build. When someone has an exciting promotion or just a new, free T-shirt, they have earned it, and they're not obligated to share anything with me. However, being a sister has made me learn to stop and think about whether I really want what they have, or if something else is prompting my envy. Here's the thing about fairness – it can't be everyone's turn, all the time. Most of the time, it won't be your turn. But you don't need to be filled with hate, jealousy or resentment about the fact that someone else is getting a go. Your moment will come.

CHAPTER TWO
Bodies and Appetites

How I'm Learning to Stop Worrying and Start Taking up More Space

When we were little, I struggled to see the similarities between my sisters and me. My biggest battle was with my body. As far as I could tell, my younger sisters had the bodies of children. Beth wasn't much younger than me, but she seemed slim and energetic. I never asked her about it, but I assumed she simply inhabited her body; it was a practical vessel that allowed her to run after things and climb up things. I also assumed that she was horribly embarrassed by her fat big sister. My body was an albatross.

I was five years old when I started to feel separate from my sisters, and other children. The only person with a body that I could identify with was Mum – she was pregnant with Livvy, and her rounded belly bloomed, as mine did. Only mine was round from thirds of lemon meringue pie. We moved to Buckinghamshire and I started a new school. In the playground I learned that I was fat, and that being fat was bad.

My body struck me as something between the result of a

witch's curse and a medical condition. I'd read *The Secret Garden,* and I loved bad-tempered Mary, who had been sent away from India and forbidden from running around like a normal child on health grounds. I could relate: I moved as though I had an imaginary bustle under my school skirt, solid and slow. Beth would run and jump, lapping me, as though she'd taken my energy and multiplied it with her own. She was a 'normal' child, and I was a freak, with a shameful secret of a body that was impossible to hide. She seemed unafraid, when I lived in fear. I was scared of getting stuck in small spaces and having to be freed by people who had been inconvenienced by my fatness. I was scared of getting up from benches and sofas, making the slimmer sitters briefly wonder whether they were airborne as I hoisted up my bulk. Most of all, I was scared of my own conspicuousness, of forgetting the limitations of my body and drawing attention to its hideousness. I felt estranged from Beth and Grace. I loved playing with them, until someone suggested that we run, or hide, or try to build a treehouse. I pretended I was above their games and buried myself in books.

It was around this time that I was sexually abused by a neighbour, an old man who had offered to look after me while my mum took care of my sisters. This was when Livvy was a seriously ill newborn baby, and Mum and Dad were spending almost all of their time in hospital with her or driving to Oxford to be with her. I believe that my parents were just as vulnerable as I was, and this wicked man took cruel advantage of the fact that they were enormously anxious, depressed and distracted.

I was alone with him when the abuse took place. As

abusers do, he told me that what happened between us was 'a secret'. I'd never had a secret from Beth before. We shared a room. We still shared a bath. I didn't have any memories that she wasn't included in, but now I had a secret that I did not want and wasn't allowed to share. This man did not invite Beth to be alone with him. I was convinced that I had been singled out because of my bad body. Being fat was dangerous, and it made me feel completely alone. My parents heard a rumour about the neighbour, and put a stop to the babysitting, but I felt deeply anxious. Surely it was only a matter of time before it happened again?

Being fat made bad things happen, so I reasoned that if I lost weight, everything would be fine. I started fantasising about being thin, the way I should have been fantasising about being a ballerina or an astronaut. I became aware of a thrilling solution – Slimfast! The adverts were enthralling, and I'd light up as Donna, 42, from Huddersfield paraded around in an old pair of trousers that now looked so enormous on her that she might as well be wearing a barrel while receiving a pardon from Abraham Lincoln. 'A Slimfast shake for breakfast, one for lunch, and a proper meal in the evening' was the very first line of poetry I ever heard. Why wasn't everyone availing themselves of this magical meal replacement plan? I'd seen the Jetsons opening silver domed dishes before tucking into protein pills. Surely eating actual food would soon be a thing of the past! Slimfast was the future!

Oddly, my parents laughed when I asked for Slimfast for my sixth birthday. I got a slide, and panicked about whether it would take my weight, or whether I'd get stuck on the steps. I thought about asking Beth to distract my parents next time we went shopping in Aylesbury, so that I could sneak some Slimfast into the trolley, but she was much more interested in trying to get hold of some Puppies In My Pocket. Well, Beth's pocket.

My relationship with food became strained. It was both the cause of and the cure for my unhappiness. I longed to lose weight, and I was sure that my failure to control my appetite was my biggest problem. If I could only be thin, the rest of my life would be bearable. But food was delicious and addictive, and when I was eating I didn't feel sad – at least, momentarily.

Most of my sisters seemed fairly indifferent to food. Beth and Grace were sometimes in trouble for not finishing their dinner, and I'd hoover up their leftovers. My 'healthy' appetite would be praised, when it was the least healthy thing about me. I was a normal, sturdy little girl, but I ate like an addict. I'd volunteer to help dish up at dinner time, in order to make sure that my portion was as large as possible. I'd eat past the point of comfort, and I'd sneak to the kitchen to fill my cheeks with leftovers when no one was looking. It was as if I'd grown up in wartime and had to consume everything within a mile radius of my mouth, just in case they brought back rationing. I was bad at sharing, but adept at getting more than my share. I was better at keeping secrets than anyone suspected, and I think my stressed, harassed parents were so focused on getting my little sisters to eat their vegetables that they didn't have the energy to worry about the fact that their eldest was eating everything in sight.

At Christmas, we'd always receive our own private stash of sweets and chocolate. Sometimes this was a selection box, but our parents tried to vary the theme so that every child received a supersized version of their favourite confectionary, or at least had something they didn't usually get to eat throughout the year. In 1993, I had my very own box of Quality Streets – a chocolate I associated with great sophistication, thinking they were much more glamorous than Roses. (We usually had a big family tin of Roses, so I guess Quality Street had some rarity value.) Beth's treat of choice was liquorice allsorts.

Beth was the first to initiate attack. I was lying on my stomach, pretending to read Polly Toynbee in the *Radio Times* while dreamily gazing at the box of Quality Street in front of me. It was made from clear plastic and shaped like a treasure chest, and I liked to covetously count the shiny wrappers. My precious casket of calorific jewels glistened under the standard lamp. Simply possessing them seemed as filling and delicious as actually eating them. I knew that once I started, I wouldn't be able to stop, and while I realised that the toxic, tearful sugar rush was inevitable, I was hoping I could postpone it by half an hour. I closed my eyes and surfed a wave of anticipation and adrenaline before I was startled back to consciousness by a chubby, grubby hand. Beth was shoving something sweet, wet and warm into my mouth.

'WHMAARGHURRRRD?' I demanded.

'Your chocolate is *disgusting*,' she replied. She'd helped herself to a peanut brittle, and on deciding it was not to her taste, decided to reunite the half-chewed chocolate with its owner. Now, Beth had plenty of evidence that I was not a fussy eater, and twenty-five years later I'm forced to admit that she was right. The peanut brittle is so disgusting that they don't bother to make it any more, and now half the box is filled with the perennially popular shiny purple prizes instead. But at the time I felt completely violated. Beth had disturbed my two sanctuaries – my chocolate hoard, and my mouth. I also couldn't understand why she refused to eat anything that didn't please her. Chocolate is chocolate.

I'd like to say that my subsequent act was one of carefully thought out revenge, but there was no malice aforethought. I was just a lonely, greedy, bored girl with a borderline sugar addiction. A few days after Christmas, I found myself alone in our shared room with Beth's big box of liquorice allsorts. Beth appeared to have eaten four or five, so the box was opened and unsealed, but almost filled to the top. What kind of weird monster still has nearly all of their Christmas sweets left on 28 December? What kind of person would leave them out, unattended, when girls like me are prowling about, unable to help themselves? Quite quickly, I convinced myself that Beth's liquorice allsorts had been left out as a personal affront. She wanted to taunt me. Just as she had absorbed all of my energy, she had all of my self-control too. I wasn't going to fall into her trap. I was just going to eat one . . . two . . . and that double-decker one, in fact I should have two more because those first two were single stacked . . . and the weird blue hundreds and thousands one, that didn't count, because it was disgusting. In twenty minutes, I had eaten all but two of Beth's allsorts.

My heart was pounding with panic and sugar. I didn't even like liquorice very much, but I was stuffed with it. It wasn't as though I could replace it. We didn't have any shops within walking distance, and I could hardly sneak out of the house without making anyone suspicious. I could stuff the box with loo roll, but that meant that my cover would be blown the second bloody Beth decided to feast on her daily single allsort ration. I felt as though I had to hide a body, and I had no alibi. All I could do was front it out. Maybe I could frame Grace.

I found Beth watching *Beauty and the Beast*, and took a deep breath. 'I have decided,' I said, pausing dramatically and puffing up my chest, which was hard to do in a woollen waistcoat, 'that I am going to help you catch the wicked liquorice allsort thief!'

'What thief?' she said, one eye still on Gaston, who was bragging about his egg consumption.

Oh, shit.

In 2015, a man named Andrew Hennells was jailed for four years after robbing a Norfolk branch of Tesco. The police found him because he posted a selfie to Facebook, in which he was holding a knife, captioned: 'Doing. Tesco. Over.' My efforts make Hennells look like a criminal mastermind. Beth ran upstairs, found her lack of allsorts and figured everything out instantly. 'Daisy, don't lie. I *know* it was you.'

'No, I saw a man leaving our room! He looked like the Milk Tray man, and he wore all black, and he had a gun, and . . .'

'You've got little bits of pink coconut around your mouth.'

'Beth, I think I have a problem.'

'Your *backside* has a problem.'*

---

* We were both mistakenly under the impression that backside was a terrible, terrible swearword, after Dad called a fellow motorist a 'pain in the FUCKING BACKSIDE!' and then said, 'I'm so sorry girls, that's a terrible word and you must promise me you will never use it.'

I cannot remember whether I was punished, but I remember that my shame covered and marked me like hot ash. Shame flamed from shin to cheek. Even my toes felt fat, and disgusting. I was a selfish, greedy little piggy who couldn't be trusted.

I felt shame again when, a few years later, Beth and I were banned from walking to the local shops with our pocket money, because we couldn't be trusted not to buy sweets. And again, in my first year at secondary school, when I skipped lunch every day for almost a week, only to binge on Boost bars from the vending machine on Friday, putting the end of one into my mouth before I'd finished the last, like a chain smoker, a mounting pile of wrappers glistening at my feet.

That was when I started making myself throw up.

My bulimia was my biggest secret of all. Mealtimes were family affairs, and any weird or inconsistent behaviour would be observed and remarked upon. Pretending everything was normal was a great challenge. I think that's why I started making myself sick. It was easier and less conspicuous than not eating during dinner.

Most of the bulimics I know started in a similar fashion. They saw an episode of *Hollyoaks* or *Grange Hill* or *Degrassi* that was devoted to the dangers of eating disorders, and while most of their brain said 'How awful!', perhaps 5 per cent filed it away as a useful tip. I've never met anyone with bulimia who came up with the idea by themselves, but I've talked to plenty who encountered the concept through a Lifetime Movie.

In the school library, I found a harrowing teen novel about a young ballerina who struggled with bulimia after a throwaway comment from her dancing teacher about her chunky thighs.

Obviously the book was intended to make its readers aware of the dangers that came with an obsession with body image. I discovered a whole genre of cautionary tales about teenage girls with eating disorders, and every single one had a name like *To the Bone* or *Dying to Be Thin*. I devoured them compulsively, as though they were chocolate biscuits. They had a pornographic quality, in that they were badly written but so thrillingly detailed. Almost every one ended with a now thin heroine, lying on a hospital bed, close to death, sometimes with the people who had bullied her when she was fat crying with remorse. I fantasised about dying in this way. Sometimes, when I was trying to concentrate on not eating lunch, I'd close my eyes and imagine lying on a bed, too weak to move, my legs like arms and my arms like fingers, while everyone I'd ever met sobbed about how they hadn't loved me enough.

Absurdly, I had a strange sense that anorexia was the more glamorous disease. I wanted to be a girl who didn't eat, and bulimia was for the days I failed, a slave to my poor impulse control, having gone without food for a paltry forty-eight hours. Perhaps the weirdest part of all was that I wanted people to worry about me, while not wanting anyone to notice me. I wanted to be *dangerously* thin. I was fed up with people saying 'you're tall for your age' or worse, *big* for my age. I hated that my bottom was too wide for some swings and slides, and that I had to pretend that I was too sophisticated for my sisters' games, when I wasn't sophisticated at all, just too wobbly to run around. I didn't want to be the eldest – the fat, jolly, bossy girl with the loud voice who corralled her sisters into order like a sergeant major. I wanted to seem breakable, to have people tiptoe and whisper and worry, to stop having to pretend to be as sturdy as I looked, not to be the biggest Russian doll in the set any more. And if I did disappear, if no one noticed that I was trying to slip through the cracks until it was too late, I would have proved that my greatest fear was true – that I wasn't loved enough.

Being at a brand new school helped, as my sisters didn't see me during the day, and any strange new aspects of my behaviour could be explained away because I was having a hard time settling in. I gamed the system. I had traintrack braces fitted and told everyone that my teeth hurt too much to chew. I threw myself into my Home Economics lessons and started learning to cook, because if I could force everyone else to try my cookies, brownies and sausage rolls, no one would know that I wasn't eating any myself. I garnered compliments and expressions of concern, and at night, I recited my declining dress sizes in my head like a countdown – '14–12–10–8–6' – a Fibonacci sequence of obsession and denial. Then Beth started to get very, very thin too.

Recently, Beth reminded me of a throwaway comment that came, improbably, from an elderly distant relative, just after I had first lost weight. 'It's funny,' he chuckled, looking at us. 'She was the fat one, and you were the scrawny one, and now you've swapped over.' I remember a brief period when Beth was fuller of face than she used to be, and evilly being quite pleased – because when you've wept over your too-big body every day and wondered why you're not more like your little sister, it's a great and strange relief when the mantle of 'the fat one' is passed along to someone else. But even though this comment had flown over my head, Beth had committed it to memory.

It has become very fashionable to complain about the excessive sensitivity of young people. However, I think this is preferable to the time in which people in their seventies and beyond were made to believe that their advanced age gave them the right to say whatever they liked to anyone they liked. They tend to say things to teenage girls, who are the most powerful yet fragile beings in existence. A teenage girl can take over the world, but if you take away her bloom of confidence with a brief burst of cruelty, you can wreck her life for years to come. And so it was with Beth. There were other factors, other bad men, other casual, cutting comments, but I believe this old man's comparing and contrasting of us both helped to make her, for a time, dangerously underweight. And she knew exactly how to make sure that her food issues went undetected because she simply had to copy me.

I wish I'd realised how much my behaviour was hurting Beth. I wish both of us had found better role models, different values, and a more useful way of understanding and appreciating our bodies. Most of all, I wish I'd told Beth how beautiful she was, and helped her to see herself properly instead of seeing her as some sort of threat. I'm ashamed of this, but there was a time when I felt thinner because Beth felt fat.

This is, I think, the worst thing about womanhood. We're told that we must hate our bodies for not conforming to certain standards, but once we've mastered the self-loathing, we're encouraged to hate other women's bodies too. Do you know a woman who was in a relationship with a man that ended because that man started a new relationship with a different woman? And did the first woman, your friend, who might speak seven languages, or be a prize-winning scientist, or a gifted comedian, say in a sad, squeaky voice, 'I hope she's not thinner than me?' Have you ever felt glee when a woman you're not particularly fond of gains weight? Have you ever lost weight specifically for a reunion or an occasion where you're going to see some old female foes, and you want to piss them off?

I've done all of these things, and I know it's not sisterly at all. Yet, it's the way in which women have been conditioned to interact with women. I have longed to inhabit my own sisters' bodies, and sometimes wished that I could make them want to inhabit mine. It's very difficult to change the shape of our story. When Bridget Jones finally gets down to her goal weight, her friends all tell her that she looks terrible, and she notes, sadly, 'I feel like a scientist who has just discovered that their life's work has been a total mistake.' For hundreds of years, we have told millions of women that the way their bodies look is much more important than whether they're clever, or funny, or kind. In fact, as women, we're not even allowed to decide that we look good; it's all about the judgements that other people make on our behalf.

Beth and I recovered, by degrees. Our teenage lives became interesting and distracting, and as we became more sure that we were liked and loved, we stopped worrying and obsessing about what not to eat. Yet, years later, when Beth became pregnant with Penelope, I noticed her food anxieties returning. Beth didn't seem to mind about the changing shape of her body, but she became preoccupied with what she was feeding the baby in her womb. She avoided milk if it had been out of the fridge for more than a few minutes. She turned down fruitcake that had absorbed a teaspoon of whisky. I understood her urge to try to take control, in the throes of a Great Unknown. But I worried that she and food had never really reached an understanding. In different ways, we were like King Canute, furiously, sweatily attempting to turn back the tide of our appetites. However, when Penny was born, Beth relaxed a little. Her beautiful baby needed to eat, and Beth found nourishment in feeding her. Practically speaking, breastfeeding wasn't always easy, but Penny reminded us that food *should* be easy. Eating is necessary, and sating your hunger makes you strong, not weak. As women, we're made to feel so frightened of having or being too much that we starve ourselves physically and sometimes emotionally. When you take away the complicated teenage toxicity, food is at the baseline of love. Babies are precious, and so are we. I realised you would never make a crying baby feel bad about being soothed with food, so I vowed to stop punishing myself over what I had for lunch.

In all honestly, I am still a disordered eater. I know my habits are not healthy, and I include them in the hope that anyone who reads this and recognises herself will seek help and make changes. I'm trying to. Most of the time I'm fine. But when I'm especially sad, stressed or anxious, I'll binge, and sometimes make myself throw up. I'll be too frightened to stop working and eat, so I will type until dinner time when I'll pretend that a main course of grilled salmon and vegetables undoes the damage of my starter, a family-sized bag of Kettle Chips. But every day, I try to remember that my worth as a woman isn't based on what I have and haven't eaten. My appetites and desires, the flavours I crave aren't unnatural. They're exciting. They make life thrilling.

A Room of One's Own

I shared a room with Beth until I was eleven. For most of our lives, I think we believed that for sisters, this was the law, and we'd still be in our twin beds, sleeping under matching Holly Hobby duvets in the old people's home. However, when we moved back to Dorset, something shifted.

Perhaps it was an early surge of adolescent hormones, but we *hated* each other. We treated each other like two tiny emperors warring over the world's smallest principality. This demonstrates the depth of my pettiness: I resented Beth looking at my Forever Friends alarm clock because I believed I owned THE TIME. More reasonably, Beth would respond with violence if I accidentally put her knickers on because they were in my drawer. Each of us thought that the bedroom was her personal space, and the sibling who slept in it was slightly less welcome than a squatter.

It didn't help that we'd moved from a fairly modern, airy house to a bigger, darker, dustier one. Even though the house was large, not all of the rooms were usable, and Mum and Dad decided that it was best if we all kept sharing until the damp problem was resolved and the roof was fixed. Our bedrooms were filled with inherited furniture and bric-a-brac. Grace and Livvy slept in bunk beds in a room dominated by a bizarre 1940s saddle-shaped exercise contraption, impossible to move because it was made of iron. They shrugged and decided it was a special tower for Beanie Babies. (The Puppy In My Pocket hotel lived on a raised driveway made from stacks of pre-war *Woman's Weekly*.) Everything was made from walnut wood, and creaked, croaked or stuck when you wanted to open it. The house was grand, but shabby, and sometimes I felt strangely ashamed of it. The previous owner had left three large glass jars which were used to store cereal. For reasons I will never understand, the lids of the jars had been decorated with a circle of badly cut lino, which was peeling away and yellow with age. Whenever friends came to visit, I'd hide the jars in a kitchen cupboard.

Beth and I were in a constant state of tense negotiation, from what went on the shiny, damask-papered walls – occasionally we'd chew each other's supply of Blu-Tack in order to make it too revolting and unsticky to support anything that the other one had ripped out of *Live and Kicking* magazine – to how we ended the day's discourse. We never went to sleep on an argument. Instead, we instigated a system where we took turns to have the last word, or the last hit. The hitter would get out of bed, smack the hittee as hard as possible and then sleep soundly, but not before muttering a soft, sneaky 'bitch' under their breath.

Mum maintains that getting my own room had a more transformative effect on my personality than going through puberty. I returned from a school trip, went to our shared room and immediately started screaming in Beth's direction. 'ALL OF MY STUFF HAS GONE! WHERE HAVE YOU TAKEN IT? WHY?' My poor, long-suffering mother separated us before blood was shed, and led me up the stairs to the top floor, and the tiny, light-filled corner room with the sloping ceilings, the windows that looked out over the hills and far away. There was my alarm clock. There was my pine cabinet, filled with cut-up copies of *Live and Kicking* (oh please let Mum not have looked at the problem pages). There was my Mickey Mouse message board. And there was a built-in wardrobe, with coat hangers in it! All for me, and only me!

My shoulders slackened and relaxed. Here, I could stay up reading as late as I liked. I could play music and put pictures on the walls. I would never find a tub of snails under the bed or walk in on someone trying on my vests and stuffing socks into them. Having this tiny pocket of space made me feel safer, and more serene. I could – and did – fall apart in that room, but it was also there that I privately worked out a way to put myself back together again. Best of all, the peeling paint was gone, replaced with beautiful blue wallpaper, the colour of sunlight shining on the bottom of a swimming pool.

The only problem with getting my own room is that it

made stealing much more difficult. I couldn't take anyone else's clothes and pretend it was an accident. We were all prolific thieves, but I'm ashamed to say that I was one of the worst perpetrators. Grace was woken up one morning by me, opening her wardrobe and selecting a shirt from a hanger – and could only splutter, 'I haven't worn that yet!'

I smiled at her unconvincing. 'You're, er, having a dream?'

I still remember clothes that I coveted more vividly than some of the clothes I owned. Beth's sheer black nylon off-the-shoulder top, decorated with scarlet velvet roses, was the most prized piece, and worth the challenge of trying to slip out of the house without her noticing me in it. In my head, it was hand-me-down payback. My sisters seemed to get plenty of new clothes – possibly more than I did – as well as all of my old ones. In my head, I was simply a stylish Robin Hood, demanding sartorial restitution.

I used to know my sisters by their stuff. When anything new entered the house, we all took a proprietorial interest, whether it was a garden table or a copy of the *Beano*. Grace's purple chenille jumper became as familiar as the front door. Most of Livvy's wardrobe was eventually repurposed as pyjamas, so she always seemed to be wearing the same thing, just at a slightly different time of day. One of the strangest, saddest things about growing up is that when my sisters and I meet at a family wedding, we'll all be wearing dresses we've never seen before, and I'll have no sense of when they bought it, why they chose it, and whether it's brand new or been seen at other parties. Sometimes I long to see Maddy and Dotty out of their avant-garde beige bodycon and back in their matching frog T-shirts, which were wiped out during the Great Toyota Previa Puking Incident of 1996. Still, this lack of familiarity means we've finally learned to respect each other's space and possessions. We've become enthusiastic lenders. I recently gave Grace the dress I wore to Beth's wedding. Livvy often has to be talked out of giving her sunglasses away to the sister who has just been admiring them.

As women, we're socialised to be ashamed of the space we take up. We're expected to be generous and accommodating, and we're told that we're not allowed to mind when someone is presumptive or intrusive. I struggle during hen parties and group holidays, when I discover, at the last minute, that I'm expected to sleep top to tail with a stranger in a single camp bed. I know some women adore these situations, and embrace the idea of being all girls together, sharing stories and cigarettes smoked through open windows. I've grown up fighting for every single square inch of space that I'm allowed to take up, and it's exhausting. I believe women flourish and thrive when they don't have to constantly compete for space but are allowed to just exist within it. Virginia Woolf championed having a room of one's own for a reason.

My sisters and I were so lucky to eventually get rooms of our own. It made our relationships stronger. It gave us a chance to feel independent and provided us with time to process our private emotions. Still, privacy has become a luxury, and it shouldn't be. In the UK, my generation is facing a housing crisis. Across the world, poverty affects women and children the most, before anyone else. What does this mean? That a room of one's own is increasingly beyond the reach of most girls and women. We all need our own space. When I wasn't forced to live in the same room as Beth, I eventually wanted to stop stealing and start giving. I could appreciate what was unique about all of my sisters, because I had undisputed territory where I could celebrate my own uniqueness too. If feminism is going to move forward, we need more room for each of us to exist in. We need to be able to shut a door and enforce a boundary every so often. We spend so much time talking about our biological clocks. Maybe, for the sake of amity, we just all need our own Forever Friends clocks.

CHAPTER THREE
The House of Puberty

'There was a point,' said my Mum, resignedly, 'when I thought that eventually, the tampons and sanitary towels would have to arrive in lorries. When I started to wonder whether I could save time and money by contacting a wholesaler, and having Lil-lets delivered on pallets every month, by the kilo.' She spoke in a tone I'd only ever heard before in documentaries about the Second World War, when bemused nonagenarians talk about what it feels like to be bombed in their beds, and still struggle to understand how they found the strength and fortitude to crack on, instead of giving up, lying down and sobbing into a crater on the pavement.

In the autumn of 2003, my parents were sharing a house with six hormonal, pubescent girls and young women – an eighteen-year-old (me), seventeen-year-old Beth, fifteen-year-old Grace, Livvy, who had just turned thirteen, and Maddy and Dotty, who were only ten but starting to experience extreme mood swings, possibly because puberty was making them feel left out, and our diva strops looked like enormous fun (unless you were Dad). 'One day, you'll all sync up!' Mum would say cheerfully, because she had no reason to doubt the magical myth of womanhood. Theoretically, if you take a group of gals and put them close to each other, they will all start menstruating at the same time, ideally when there's a new moon. What actually happened was that on any given day, one of us would be threatening everyone else with a bread knife, one of us would be lying upside down across the stairs with her legs in the air, screaming for a hot water bottle, one of us would be systematically emptying the kitchen cupboards, starting with the good stuff and ending with stale cooking chocolate that predated the millennium, and the rest would be laughing at everyone else or napping.

I'd read every Judy Blume book that the local library stocked (although I couldn't find the sexy one, *Forever*, and I daren't ask, even though the stern, silver-haired lady behind the counter was constantly reading Mills and Boon series that appeared to be called *The Oiled Nipple Chronicles*) and as a result, I was quite excited about getting my period. It would be a badge of maturity that would make sense of my weird, too-big body. Various aunties and relatives were always telling me, in slightly weary tones, that I was mature for my age. Getting my period early was the prize I deserved for a lifetime of being good, sensible and boring. I was top of my English class, never late with homework and one of the only people who could be trusted to wheel the Acorn computers into the hall without jumping on the trolley and riding them into the wall. Menses would be my reward! After my tenth birthday, I looked for my period every time I went to the loo, as if it were a rare gorilla, and I was Sigourney Weaver. Every so often, I'd produce blood with a particularly pointy poo, and leap up to tell Mum.

Over the years, I've asked a lot of my mother, and she

has responded to some appalling requests with great grace. She's done my laundry, bailed me out when I've gone over my overdraft and driven me seventy miles across the country, waited in the car while I failed a flute exam and then driven me seventy miles home. Still, I think her most generous act as a parent has probably been patiently and repeatedly explaining the difference between menses blood, and blood from my anus. 'I'm sure it's coming any day now!' she'd beam, her face not betraying the horror she must have felt at the possible prospect that it might not come any day, and that I could be well into my teens before she could stop telling me that it wasn't a period, just a poo.

Finally, the great moment came, during a rehearsal for a school production of *Robin Hood*. Beth and I were playing children of Sherwood, and we had starring roles. After the first scene, Beth said, 'Quick, the sheriff is coming!' and I said, 'Oh no!' while pointing at the audience and cueing their boos, as if the sheriff were lurking among them and nicking their Revels. At the rehearsal I felt out of sorts, and I knew that it wasn't just because I'd been secretly hoping that someone had made a mistake, and I was actually meant to be Maid Marian. Beth was being really annoying, but usually I could pinpoint the exact source of this annoyance and share it with her. ('Stop breathing!' 'You're being *near me*.' 'Please stop singing that song from the yoghurt advert, I will *wee on your head* next time I hear Mmm, Danone!) But I felt edgy, twitchy and indefinably cross. I wanted to blame Beth for secretly slicing my skin off, coating my organs with sand and then sewing the skin back on without me realising. But I didn't know how to articulate this uncomfortable sensation, and even I couldn't invent a reason for accusing Beth of being involved.

At home, I went to the loo and locked the door, wanting to be alone with my sulk. Now, I grew up with an absolutely enormous privilege, and this is probably the main reason why my sisters and I made it to adulthood without committing sororicide. When we moved to Dorset, we moved to a house that had four loos. The downstairs one, which was relatively secluded, looked out onto a restful sylvan tableau. It was a large room, and its supporting wall was made from built-in cupboards, and the storage facilities were well used. You'd never run out of loo roll and, if you knew where to look, you could find a secret stash of *Viz* annuals, as long as you were prepared to shut the toilet seat and stand on it on your tiptoes. In addition, at Christmastime, you could do some serious present snooping. If anyone suspected you were up to something and banged on the door, you just shouted, 'Go away! This is a *very complicated poo*!' The only trouble was that this was the loo visitors were directed to, so there was always a risk that you'd announce your imaginary bowel movement, then open the door and find yourself face to face with an alarmed parish priest.

Mum and Dad's en suite had two doors – one opening into their room, and one opening into the room the twins shared. This toilet was no good at all, unless you liked to wee while fearing imminent ambush. The one on the top floor of the house was cold, populated by those 'harmless' house spiders that are big enough to have visible eyelashes and elbows, and festooned with passive-aggressive cartoon cautionary tiles that had been left in place by the previous owner, and not removed. (One had a poem about not leaving wet towels on the floor. You'd wet your towels too, if you'd just been surprised by a spider with elbows.)

So, for the family Buchanan, 'the end bathroom' was our safe space. It was the last room on the top floor, at the end of a very long corridor, next to nothing but a grumbling Edwardian boiler that could be trusted to keep your secrets safe. Just as the Mitfords had their Hons Cupboard, the linen closet where confidences were exchanged and misdeeds were confessed, we had our end bathroom. It was where broken hearts were mended, arguments were resolved, and where we learned the secrets of the universe from back copies of the *Reader's Digest*. It was a safe, slightly smelly womb, and the very best place for me to start my transition into womanhood. I sat down, sighed, and picked up a classic 1989 *RD*. I was about to start reading 'Not tonight, dear! Does she *really* have that headache?' when I noticed that the crotch of my M&S knickers was a slightly muddy red. I'd been expecting a shock of scarlet, for my evolving body to announce that dramatic changes were taking place in unignorable neon. This was much softer and more subdued than I believed it would be, entrails blooming in dirt.

Suddenly and delightedly, I knew I had a semi-decent reason for wanting to murder everyone I knew – an urge that dissolved the moment I could name it. I yelled, 'MUM!' She heard from the opposite end of the house. 'I absolutely knew what had happened, the second I heard your voice,' she told me later, which was touching and tender and deeply reasonable, given she had every right to say, 'Are you sure this isn't another poo?'

Periods were a brilliant opportunity for bossiness. After my first period I knew everything, and if I didn't I could make it up. 'During your period, you have to eat sunflower seeds!' I shouted at Beth, when she had yet to start and did not want to know. (Mum had taken me to the local health food shop for snacks after establishing that catering packs of Maltesers might be both the cure and the cause of my cramps.) 'This is because . . .' I said, trying very hard to think of something sensible and logical, 'erm . . . when your body releases an egg, you become biologically compatible with . . . hamsters, and you must copy their diet. This is why I need to eat this two-kilogram bag of seeds, and why you can't have any.'

Beth glowered at me. 'I don't care. I'm never going to start my periods, ever, because only losers like you get them.'

About a year later, I was getting ready for school and I heard a muffled sobbing sound coming from Beth's room. I knocked. The sobbing stopped for a few seconds, and then I heard a lone, frustrated howl. 'Beth?' I heard heavy exhalation, and then there was silence. I pushed open her door, which was sticky and slightly swollen in its frame, which made it *very difficult* to sneak up on Beth when she was in her natural habitat. You could only ever burst in on her, like a sitcom character who was about to make someone else the victim of their hilarious misunderstanding. Beth was in the wardrobe. The base wasn't quite wide enough for her to sit down, so she'd bent her body awkwardly, like an umbrella handle, her head and shoulders curved and shoved under a shelf. The people who used to live in our house probably kept their hats there, fifty years ago. I wasn't sure how Beth had got into the wardrobe, but the bigger and more complicated question was how to get her out. Emotionally, I was confident that it would be a piece of cake, but practically speaking, we were going to need a hammer.

'Don't tell Mum,' sobbed Beth, and I feared the worst. She was being expelled. She had sleep-killed Grace and hidden the body in the playhouse at the bottom of the garden. She'd accidentally watched a forbidden episode of *Neighbours* and was holding a vigil for her own immortal soul. 'I've started my period.'

By then, I was a veteran – which meant I knew where the sanitary towels were kept, and I was not sufficiently sensitive to Beth's distress. 'Don't be silly, you just need some paracetamol! Now, come out of the wardrobe and stop being a twat.' Beth cried harder. 'Mum will be really pleased!' I said, because Mum had given me the impression that she was genuinely delighted her eldest daughter was now permanently spotty, greasy, furious, and on the brink of becoming addicted to over-the-counter painkillers. I tried to hug Beth, through a maze of wire coathangers, and she cried for a little bit longer before falling out of the wardrobe.

I don't know why we felt so differently about our periods. When I started, I think I saw it as another validation of my big sister status – but maybe Beth felt differently because they made her less of a little sister. I was in a hurry to assume grown-up trappings, and she wanted to stay little for a little bit longer.

Beth did not follow my second instruction. Puberty transformed her into an entirely new kind of twat. Instead of being my bullied, put-upon, best friend by default, she started to show signs of independent thought. How very dare she? Instead of begging to borrow my Vengaboys single, she was rolling her eyes at everything I did and said, and cursing me for being 'mainstream'. 'You're such a *slave to the man*,' she'd sigh, as she watched me put milk in my tea, or try to find a clean pair of socks. 'Who cares about your socks, really? Society! With its bourgeois values of cleanliness!'

I cared about my socks, simply because I didn't want to force anyone to phone up a fumigator every time I took my shoes off. Puberty was testing my own bourgeois values of cleanliness, simply by making me really, really stinky. At school, I was nicknamed 'Hitler' because of the very precise, restrained way I put my hand up in class. This unfortunate trademark came about because I needed to keep my arm clamped close to my body, and hide the fact that Soft and Gentle roll-on was no match for my Hard and Angry armpit. I'd embraced womanhood with alacrity, and where had it got me? I had a newly furious sister who hated me even more than she hated it when people accidentally called her a goth, and a body that, among other things, smelled like a fridge that has just been opened after a fortnight's holiday and a power cut. Beth used to hug me in the halls at school, and I'd push her away, saying, 'Urghh, get off, people will think we're *lesbians*!' Now she ignored me, especially if she was with her new friends, and she wouldn't even let me borrow her cool new hoodies ('You've never heard of Less Than Jake and you'll stretch it with your vast, cowlike boobs!').

It seemed as though puberty was setting me apart from my sisters, but it was the tits that did it, really. I could put up with any amount of cramping, random violent rage or suddenly sprouting hair as long as I didn't have to deal with two huge, visible clues that I was different from my siblings. At least one myth didn't come true. When magazines and adverts made vague, unqualified references to 'managing your bikini line', I thought it meant that two lines of pubes would appear across each breast, meeting in the middle like a reverse pencil tit goatee. In preparation for that dark day, I stockpiled polo necks and excuses about why I could never go on another family holiday ever again.

It didn't seem fair, at all, that Beth could go through puberty and be relatively untroubled by breasts. In fact, it was the same for all of my sisters. Everyone seemed to have enough going on to graduate from a training bra, but no one else was chased by men yelling 'You don't get many of those to the pound!' because they had the temerity to wear a sleeveless T-shirt on a hot day. I had two options. Again, there was the polo neck one, or I could choose to define myself by my boobs, which made me Not Beth. She got to be pale and interesting, pretty and artistic. I got to be Babs Windsor. My sisters *still* hate playing Monopoly with me because if anyone gets a Community Chest card I shout, 'That's me!'

Even though my breasts shrank down to nearly nothing when I was anorexic, they popped straight back up the moment I started eating cheese again. I suddenly looked as though I was shoplifting Christmas puddings under my jumper. 'The boys are back in towwwwwwn!' I'd sing, trying to motorboat myself while everyone else took advantage of the fact that I was temporarily blinded by my own nipples, and left the room. Puberty made me sexy. Wait, that's a lie. Puberty made me believe that being sexy was very important, and that there was no point trying to be subtle about it, because it was vital to convince as many people as possible that you were a hot piece of ass. I'd make cruel fun of Grace, whose favourite piece of clothing was a purple chenille jumper. 'No one would fancy you in that!' I'd sneer, hoping my meanness would soothe my soul after having a screaming match with Mum, because she wouldn't let me wear a diamante fuschia New Look nylon bustier out of the house.

It was a very confusing time. I was aware that my body was playing tricks on me, and I seemed deeply unappealing – every part of me was either smelly, bleeding or covered in blackheads. Yet, being the slightly surprised owner of Really Big Tits brought me strange and unignorable amounts of attention. It was as though I was followed everywhere by a billion-pound Jeff Koons balloon dog sculpture. Most people were frighteningly positive, a few were volubly upset, but everyone had something to say, and they were keen to shout it loudly. Puberty had brought me a very inconvenient superpower. Less of an invisibility cloak, more of a Screaming Attention Tabard. I wanted my sisters to envy the tabard, because I envied them their freedom. It shames me to realise that at the time, I didn't realise that their bodies were giving them just as much trouble and confusion as mine was. It didn't occur to me to be anything but envious, or to think about what they might be struggling with below the surface. I needed to keep validating myself, loudly and obnoxiously, in order to silence the sneaky murmur that kept whispering that I might not have anything to validate. Puberty gave me a personality! We all had our hobbies and interests. Dotty liked Pokémon, Maddy was the gossipy sister, Liv was super sociable, Grace was into science, Beth was arty and I was the one with the wabs.

I worked out that my body and brain were out of sync when I was twelve, and on an awkward family holiday. We were in northern France. We were *always* in northern France, staying in farmhouses and surrounded by furious-looking cows, as the paying guests of men and women with tiny eyes and rigid hair who would count the forks at the end of the fortnight, while we children sat squashed under luggage, with the car engine running. We visited Bayeux, which, boringly, had the long, dull, famous tapestry, and thrillingly, a tiny branch of New Look. Beth and I would run around the tapestry with unseemly haste, and if we correctly answered some tapestry trivia (to which the answer was always 'William the Conqueror', or '1066') we were allowed to dash off and spend our sticky francs on glittery hair clips and crop tops that we wouldn't be allowed to wear outdoors. Then, clutching bags of rubber bracelets and Conqueror key rings, we'd go to a local restaurant with a dark dining room, where our poor parents would try to persuade us to eat something slightly French before giving up and ordering omelettes jambon et frites, pour six.

We ran in a pack. We were a rainbow of childishness, with me at the beginning, chubby and ruddy, and Maddy and Dotty at the end, often in some sort of violet, violent sulk. We ate the same things. We looked the same. We were six bratty English children, separate from our long-suffering parents, and the only difference between us was that some of us were slightly longer than others.

So one lunch, I was horrified when the waiter walked

behind me, the last of the group to leave the restaurant, and pinched my bum.

I was wearing a black cotton dress that must have become slightly rucked as I got up from my chair – enabling the waiter to touch my flesh under the fabric. I remember the shock of the pinch, the grip of his fingers and the way it took me whole seconds to realise that this wasn't Mum tugging my skirt down or bustling me out of the building. This was a stranger. And I remember how quickly that shock turned to shame, the speed with which my blood rose to the surface of my skin, the nausea, the panic, the sense that quite by accident, I had done something deeply wrong. Beth's advice was 'Don't tell Dad', so I didn't. I never wore that dress again, and seemed to spend the rest of the holiday floating in space. I had a horrible secret that was too grown up to share with the grown-ups. In my head and in my heart, I felt just like my sisters – even though I was bossy, superior and controlling, we were all part of the same clan. Yet my body had started to make me separate. The waiter had waited for me to leave, before pouncing upon me. I thought I was still a child but I'd invoked a horribly adult response from him.

For years, I wouldn't let myself think about the incident. No one pinched my bum when I was anorexic. I'd tried so hard to make my body ignorable, and shrink it down to nothing, but my efforts weren't sustainable. Apart from the mood swings and constant fainting, I was just too hungry all the time. If I couldn't reduce my flesh sufficiently, I'd simply have to grow my personality in order to make it match. Besides, I was a crap Catholic. If I couldn't be good, I might as well be very, very bad. Maybe I wanted to have my bum pinched by strangers, if only to prove that it was pinchable!

I thank my lucky stars that in my efforts to become a big-time seductress, I was mostly playing to an audience of nervous virgins wearing fleeces. Also, I am very fortunate that I decided to become a self-described slut before the internet really got going and my attempts were not assisted by Tinder. Finally, my would-be promiscuity was hampered by the fact that I was basing my efforts on a really pulpy biography of Jean Harlow, and the availability of cheap fishnet hold-up stockings in the big Leeds Primark. I wasn't so much the sort of girl that could make a bishop kick a hole in a stain-glass window as one who could make a second-year History student hide in the loos of Oceana for twenty minutes.

Psychologists have claimed that the state of adolescence doesn't really end at eighteen or nineteen, and mental health guidelines now recommend that young people are treated as teenagers up until the age of twenty-five. I feel as though that's how long it took me to go through puberty, and my body – and my relationship with it – was tumultuous and unsettled until my mid-twenties. I wish it hadn't felt so frightening. I wish I hadn't given so much weight to the reactions of strangers, and that I hadn't wasted so much time trying to become invisible, then extra visible. Most of all, I wish that I hadn't felt so separate from my sisters during that time. I was so worried that puberty would make me different from them, forever, but ultimately we all had to go through it, and we could have made it easier for each other if we'd felt less isolated by it and shared more.

Women are formed in volcanoes. There's a point in our young lives when we're all transformed by huge amounts of strange physical pressure. I think it's what makes us so strong, because we're all forged by force. We're all attempting to survive the world in bodies that sometimes feel borrowed, and less comfortable than the scratchy, unflattering jumpers that well-meaning distant relatives give us at Christmas. We're all sisters in spirit when we've all blinked uncomprehendingly at the instructional leaflets that come with boxes of Tampax, or wondered why our breasts seem to point in slightly different directions, or gone into the bathroom with a pair of tweezers to sort out our eyebrows and emerged, dazed, after ninety minutes, plucked from navel to knee.

Womanhood can feel like a permanent state of physical chaos, but it's chaos that unites us. I think we have a responsibility to remind each other that while the blood, hair and strange smells are inevitable and endurable, the bum-pinching is not. Puberty isn't a process that's supposed to make us feel resigned to our fates, but one that reminds us to be tough for each other. We might feel, at points, as though we don't have total control of our bodies. But we can come together and call out anyone who can't control their response *to* our bodies.

CHAPTER FOUR
Once a Catholic

For me, the nicest thing about growing up Catholic was that I had a solid, tangible reason for everything about my family that seemed completely insane. Families – even, I believe, unhappy ones – are intense and codependent little gangs. It doesn't matter how many battles you fight amongst yourselves, you're united in your war against the outside world. Although, to be fair, our war was very one-sided. We – or rather, our parents – raged against pierced ears, rap music, Sky TV, anklets, *Sweet Valley High* books, eyeshadow, Madonna (formerly one of ours!) and the film *Mrs Doubtfire* because someone said 'shit' in it. Even treats like Diet Coke and ketchup were suspect. While Mum permitted them at the table, her infernal inferences suggested that Satan probably liked to smother his food in red sauce, and we should be very careful, because pleasure would corrupt us, and he wouldn't think twice about stealing our souls if we volubly relished the delicious E numbers.

Loving the Father, the Son and the Holy Ghost was a full-time job. We never forgot we were Catholic, and we certainly weren't allowed any time off from it. My sisters and I had to contemplate it every single morning – not through prayer, but because everyone else at school wanted to talk about what happened in *Neighbours*, and that was forbidden viewing. Every week, I listened intently at Mass, desperately hoping that the priest would mention some sort of spiritual loophole that meant it was imperative that we caught up on the adventures of Toadfish and Annalise. Every week, I was disappointed.

It took me some time to realise that Catholic doctrine didn't explicitly ban Australian soaps, or tops that showed your belly button. But it was easier to assume that it did, and at least we had an umbrella term for that which seemed to separate us from every other child in the known universe. Still now, I divide the world into what is Catholic, and what isn't. BBC2 is quite Catholic. Thick, stripy jumpers are Catholic, *especially* if they don't end at your waist, and go all the way over your bum. Yet, cardigans are more Catholic than jumpers. Baileys is the most Catholic drink, or if you want to be the most Catholic you can have a Baby Guinness, which is a shot of Tia Maria with a Baileys top.

Blur were more Catholic than Oasis,* *even though* the Vatican put *What's the Story (Morning Glory)?* on an official Catholic Church playlist in 2010. All-Bran is more Catholic than Bran Flakes. For a time, my parents subscribed to a weekly newspaper called *The Universe*, which featured an 'interview' with an improbable Catholic celebrity. Spiritual credentials were abandoned in pursuit of big, A-list names.

---

* As an adult, I have reversed my position here. Blur sing sardonically about a pastoral wonderland, and their ironic detachment is *pure* C of E. Oasis, for the first three albums at least, are blood, guts, tears, fights, smoke, drama and a sense of having nothing to lose. Eventually I learned that 'Catholic' is not shorthand for 'that which is slightly less cool than the alternative, and probably wears a thick, buttoned cardigan'.

You never saw Gloria Hunniford or Sister Wendy in *The Universe*, but it wasn't unusual to catch Johnny Depp, Gwyneth Paltrow or the White Stripes, who, the newspaper claimed, were named after the sweets they were given as children for being good during Mass. (My sisters and I tried to form a band on this basis, but we gave up after arguing about whether we'd be called the Freddoes or the Capri-Suns.)

The most Catholic shop was Past Times, a retailer that specialised in Victorian nightgowns, audio books about Brother Cadfael, tiny works of Charles Dickens rendered in marzipan, and handy wooden bridges, designed to go over the small ornamental moats that millions of catalogue subscribers seemed to have in their gardens. (Past Times went into administration, and I'm sure it's connected with the decline of the ornamental moat.) When I read Zadie Smith's novel *The Autograph Man*, I nearly cried with shock. Alex-Li Tandem, the protagonist, makes long lists just like mine, only his divide everything in the world into 'Jewish' and 'Goyish'. Religion makes you see the world in a weirdly binary way.

There is a part of the Catholic Mass in which the congregation is asked to 'reject the glamour of Satan'. Do you know how *hard* it is to reject the glamour of Satan? Of course, that's the whole point of Satan. No one ever said it was going to be easy to get to heaven – camels and needles and all that. But every single Mass, I'd hold my breath, enthralled and appalled by the fact that this Satanic glamour was about to get a reference, and frightened that my face would betray my interest in what might be on offer. I got a break from this torture once I turned sixteen and started having sex. The focus of my anxiety became the moment in the Apostles Creed in which everyone says that Jesus was 'born of the Virgin Mary', and my face would flame crimson, as I looked straight ahead and hoped everyone would think that the heaters had suddenly come on.

I truly believed that Satan would turn up on a motorbike, in leather leggings, looking like someone who got his big break shifting amps for Def Leppard. I would have to say 'NO THANK YOU SATAN!' and make the sign of the cross while tugging my unflattering Aran jumper even further over my bum, when I longed to leap on the back of the bike, and immediately become wickedly sexy and leathery, Olivia Newton-John in the last ninety seconds of *Grease*. Worrying about sneaky Satan was all-consuming. I thought about it a bit more than I thought about what might go wrong if I forgot to shut a country gate, and a bit less than I feared burning the house down in case I had to light a match during a power cut.

Above all, being Catholic made me anxious. I knew the world was filled with bad people, who wanted nothing better than to provide me with opportunities to be bad too. I had to be endlessly vigilant and fretful, in order to prove that I was good and pure, just like Brother Cadfael, who loomed large in my life. (For the uninitiated, Cadfael is a fictional monk who solves murder mysteries.) Even when my sisters were mean to me (and I'd always be mean right back), I had a vague idea that they weren't just young, bratty and dickish, but that they were testing me to see whether I'd ever get to heaven by turning the other cheek like Jesus. Instead of turning the other cheek I'd try to punch them in the face, failing every time. At least there was nothing glamorous about it.

The sin of hitting your sisters was a comfortingly obvious

one. I knew exactly which rule I had contravened, and I had something specific to say in the confessional booth after 'Bless me father, for these are my sins'. I'd pad it out with 'and my parents are probably very disappointed with me'. Once, I confessed to the sin of getting four marks out of twelve in a surprise test about the Victorian railway system, as I got distracted by the romance of the name 'Darlington'. The people of Darlington, I imagined, would dress themselves in foaming frills. Instead of walking, they would float meditatively under parasols, stopping for an occasional ice cream sundae.

The night before a trip to confession, I'd lie awake, counting my sins and wondering whether I'd go to hell for forgetting any – or whether I'd accidentally get carried away and confess to something I'd seen someone else do on TV, and get carted to a police cell. I mean, just *watching The Bill* was probably a sin. I'd not seen enough of it to understand what GBH actually was, but that wouldn't necessarily stop me from panicking and confessing to it.

Mum was annoyingly vague and confusing when I asked for reassurance. 'What you say in that booth is completely confidential. The priest isn't allowed to tell *anyone.* Even if a murderer goes in and confesses to murder, the priest can't call the police.'

I thought for a second. 'So you and Dad can't go to Father Leary and say, "Tell me what Daisy said"?'

Mum frowned. 'Why? What have you done?'

When I started going to confession, shortly after my seventh birthday, I had done something bad. Really, really awful. It was so terrible that I couldn't even confide in Beth.

It was the fault of my best friend Jessica, who had invited me to her house after school and made me watch her take off her Beach Barbie's gold bikini, lie her down on a Kleenex box that had been covered with a pillowcase, and place Ken on top of her. Jessica turned to me solemnly. 'Now they're having sex,' she explained, adding, 'but you're not supposed to know what sex is until you're sixteen. It's against the law.'

There it was! The glamour of Satan! For less than half a second, I felt a giddy thrill at being initiated into the adult world. Then I burst into tears. 'Against the law!' I wailed. 'We're going to prison.'

Jessica started weeping too. 'I know, I know,' she sobbed. 'I had to tell you because I thought that at least we could go to prison together.'

During the day, I could forget what I knew, but at night, I'd lie awake in bed, trying to breathe as soundlessly as possible, and wait for the police to knock at the door, while Mum and Dad watched *Poirot*. I imagined officers tumbling out of a van, like clowns, battering their way in with truncheons. I thought about the way the handcuffs would feel, cold and heavy, cutting into my plump wrists, being led down the stairs in my nightie while Dad said, 'Lock her up forever! We never want to see her again! We're *so ashamed*.'

Every time I went to confession, I thought about confessing the sin of knowing about sex, but I wasn't entirely convinced that Father Leary wouldn't immediately notify both police and parents, perhaps via the Pope. 'Hello? John Paul? Yeah, I know about the clergy–penitent privilege, but this girl has done something *really bad*, I thought I should ask you . . . a dispensation? Sure, I'll notify the authorities straight away.'

As the months went by and the law enforcement officers didn't come, I'd just about convinced myself that my prosecution would be a waste of everyone's time and money. But I still couldn't make myself forget what I knew. Confession was meant to be a rebirth, an Etch-a-Sketch shakedown that left you pure and unmarked. But my unconfessable sin marked me, and no amount of spiritual Tipp-Exing could completely conceal my inherent badness.

I tried so very hard to be good, but as I got older, I became worse and worse. I was constantly committing unexpected sins. Using words that definitely weren't proper swears, that appeared in books and on TV without causing consternation, like 'bitchy' or 'gob', definitely counted as sinning. Bitching itself was a sin, which puzzled me – I wasn't being rude to anyone's face, and I was simply judging them for failing to rise to the moral code I was almost killing myself to meet. Then there was the sin of impure thoughts. So you could go to hell for simply not liking someone, in your head, or for liking them *too much*. Life was a minefield. You'd be better off dead, only you really wouldn't, because a lifetime of accidentally using the wrong words or thinking the wrong things would condemn you to an eternity of pitchfork-themed damnation.

It got much, much worse. I discovered wanking.

Later, I learned that Beth was told about the facts of life somewhere in the playground, and the account was much more graphic but the consequences of that knowledge were prison-free. Sensible Beth thought, 'Urghhh, that sounds absolutely revolting, I never want to think about that again. I shall focus my energies on training my racing snails, because my odd hobby is going to become a legitimate sport any day now.'

But my horror of shame, sin and bodies was tinged with prurience. What would it feel like to be naked, and have someone lie on top of you? It must feel good. It must be something people wanted to do; after all, every magazine I saw on the shelf at Sainsbury's had something to do with sex on the cover. None of them led with the coverline 'How to murder more people', so sin-wise, surely sex couldn't be all that bad?

Almost by accident, I realised that touching myself felt good, while knowing instinctively and immediately that it must be very, very bad. The problem reached a climax, as it were, when I was thirteen and Beth was twelve, and we were confirmed. I still remember the three-month fight I had with Mum about my confirmation dress. I was thrilled by the promise of a new outfit and had set my heart on a gorgeously unsuitable dress from River Island: pink, thick damask silk with spaghetti straps, and a slit that rose to the thigh. I was confirmed in a floor-length, button-down oatmeal dress with a collar. I wanted a look that screamed 'Hello boys' and ended up with one that murmured 'Blessed be the fruit'. Beth got a modish suedette lilac frock that stopped above the knee, partly because her body still looked like a child's, and didn't need to be hidden. I'd never hated her harder, and I could feel my acid envy from my toes to my fingertips.

As a confirmation gift, I was given a book of masses and prayers adorned with a photo of my old adversary, Pope Jean Paul II. That night, before bed, I opened the book and prayed that this was the start of a new and extremely Catholic chapter in my life, that I would find grace, live without sin, and become a pure, shiny respectable human. Lord, make me chaste, *immediately.* I read a Pope paragraph four times. It didn't make any sense. I thought about touching myself. I read the Pope paragraph a fifth time. Then I closed the book, got out of bed, and put the Pope in my wardrobe, face down, under a pile of old schoolbags. I got back into bed, made myself come, and then cried myself to sleep.

I was starting to feel a little bit lost. Getting confirmed was supposed to guide me back to the path I kept straying from. Why was I so, so bad at being good? I was the token teenager in the house, and I was struggling to work out what that meant, or who I was supposed to be. Following the rules was hard, but it seemed easier than dealing with my darkness, my random bouts of extreme sadness, and my utter confusion about who I was and what I was doing. At school, I was a weird, earnest little goody-goody, a B-list pal who could make people laugh, but was always left on the outside when everyone else in the class was meant to be pairing up. At home, I was a hormonal monster who was constantly saying the wrong thing, at war with everyone and affronting God with my very existence. I was alone, and I was very lonely, so I read. I discovered that my tastes were, in the true sense of the word, catholic.

In the school library, I binged, back to back, on every single Tennessee Williams play I could get my hands on. I constructed worlds I couldn't completely understand. The words made me feel understood and nourished in a way I didn't know how to articulate. Like Laura Wingfield, I longed to entertain a gentleman caller, but I was certain that the right one would never come. *Camino Real* went straight over my head, but I could sense the heat, the stickiness, the mysticism. This was Catholicism, gone gorgeously, gloriously weird, and in my gut it made much more sense to me than the anglicised, buttoned-up, literal interpretation.

I discovered Anita Brookner, and inhaled *Look at Me*, finding a kinship with the outsider heroine Frances that had eluded me in every other friendship and relationship I'd ever experienced. I'd spent my life feeling as though I were leaning over the landing bannisters, eavesdropping on conversations I couldn't understand and wasn't supposed to know about, and Frances seemed to be stuck in the same miserable realm as me. In Jane Austen's *Mansfield Park*, I met one of her namesakes, Fanny Price, and lost my heart to another girl who seemed to feel exactly as I did, 'exceedingly timid and shy, shrinking from notice'. I was exhausted from pretending *not* to be timid, and Fanny felt like a fictional sister; again, someone who would understand exactly how I felt if only she was real and knew me. As an adult I occasionally meet women who think Fanny is a gutless, wet waste of space and I feel a little bit betrayed by them. Having skipped ahead several grades in my sentimental education, I got into *Sweet Valley University* before I started *Sweet Valley High*. To my shock and joy, the Wakefield twins and their friends were having admittedly fairly angsty intercourse, but no one immediately gets pregnant, or drowns in a well. And then, I met Armistead Maupin.

Tales of the City lived on a bookcase in the spare room, a bedroom on the first floor of the house that was always referred to by the descriptor 'spare', not 'guest', even though it

was kept spare for the purpose of having guests to stay, and it
wasn't really spare at all, when the twins were sharing a room
at the time, and I can't quite remember where Livvy slept.
The spare room was full of 'bad' books – or rather, dark,
funny, sexy, thrilling books in which characters led lives that
contravened everything I had ever been taught about how a
good girl ought to live. In the spare room, I became
intimately involved with Bret Easton Ellis, Mary Gaitskill,
Virginia Andrews, Grace Metalious and, oddly, Lynne Perrie,
who played Ivy Tilsley in *Coronation Street* and who put her
name to a book called *Secrets of the Street*. (One detail that
will stay with me for life is the passage of the book where she
describes confusing Vaseline with Vicks VapoRub, and using
the latter as an erotic lubricant, to her husband's eye-watering
alarm. I believe that Lynne's book served as a cautionary tale
that improved the sex lives of all of her readers.)

I think I picked up *Tales of the City* after shuddering my
way through *American Psycho*, a horror story so hyperbolic it
shouldn't be frightening – but it really is. I tried to ape
Patrick Bateman's ironic detachment, but because I knew I
shouldn't have been reading it, I couldn't tell anyone about
how freaked out I was by Ellis's descriptions of dismembered
sex workers.

Tales was, unlike the sensation of Vicks VapoRub on your
privates, a soothing balm. It's seemingly the story of Mary
Ann Singleton, a secretary who runs away from Cleveland in
order to find herself among the fabulous freaks of seventies
San Francisco. But it's really all about Michael Tolliver, and
his great passions and vulnerabilities, and his capacity for
romance and tenderness.

It was the first love story I read that was about boys and boys, not boys and girls. I didn't know anyone who was gay – well, of course I did, but I didn't know anyone who was out. Two girls in sixth form were rumoured to be dating, and someone said they'd been caught having sex in a computer lab. I joined the chorus, claiming it was 'disgusting', making out that I was horrified by these girls and their display of lust and desire. Pathetically, I didn't speak up in their defence, because I was frightened of what would happen if I went against public opinion, and scared that anyone would associate me with any kind of sex at all.

But Michael Tolliver, who wasn't even real, seemed so kind and true, and so deserving of love, that I couldn't keep subscribing to the idea that any relationship that isn't sanctioned by the Bible could be wrong. Armistead Maupin had created a world in which love and sex were everyone's greatest motivations. The bad, wrong sex happened between characters who were greedy, angry or unhappy. The joyful, happy sex happened when people really liked the people they were having sex with. That book loosened a stitch on the moral hair shirt I'd been knitting for myself over hundreds of Sundays of Mass. Surely no one as wonderful and kind as Michael could be condemned to hell because of simple, mutual desire? And if he deserved a happy sex life, so did I.

For a long time, my life felt very dark and sad, because I was constantly scared of doing something wrong and going to hell. Ironically, these books made me feel closer to heaven. They let the light in. When I was desperately lonely, I found friends – it didn't matter that I would never meet them, or that they didn't exist; they shared themselves generously. I learned that there are millions of ways to live and to be, and that you can't possibly have any adventures unless you open yourself up to them all, rather than following a very specific path outlined by one book, written thousands of years ago. I travelled for miles from the spare room, all over America and around Europe, and I met girls like me who had survived lives like mine, whose rebellions were celebrated, not punished.

Sometimes my sisters and I communicate through books, when we can't find enough words. I didn't know how to keep reminding Livvy that being a teenager in a houseful of rules is a seemingly endless hell – but it *does* end, so I gave her every single Marian Keyes book and hoped that the Walsh sisters would succeed where I had failed. One joyous fortnight in France, I became closer to Grace than ever because, about five years after everyone else in the world, I started reading *Harry Potter* and I adored it as much as she did. The best thing about falling in love with a book is that your relationship with it is separate and unique, but when someone else loves it too, you're not envious and jealous of their love – you only love each other more.

The idea that a book might have the answers is a religious one. I believe that every book has *an* answer for us. Reading will keep us curious and compassionate, kind and alive. Reading will stop us from ever making our minds up. I hope there's a heaven, and I hope it's full of writers, because everyone who has ever made a sad person laugh, or reached out to a lonely person in the middle of the night in the dark is a person who deserves eternal joy. Reading has made me better and braver, and I think I'm a reader before I am a writer.

Beth

Beth baffles me. I love her to the end of everything, in a consuming, suffocating way. The sensation has sometimes felt like swallowing a school fête-sized bouncy castle, and having someone else inflate it through my oesophagus. Yet, and I can't stress this strongly enough, I've had more violent urges towards her than I've had with the rest of my sisters put together.

When we were very little, I thought of the pair of us as cubs, always nestling together, jostling for space, making each other feel cosy but claustrophobic, one reaching while the other wriggled away. I don't remember a day of my life in which she didn't exist. I have done things to Beth that would get me sent to prison if I did them now to a stranger on the street – biting, screaming, swearing, slamming small fingers within the frames of heavy doors. My therapist has told me, patiently and repeatedly, that we are responsible for the way we feel and no one makes us feel anything. Most of the time, I believe her, but Beth is totally capable of making me feel things. She makes me tense, defensive, insecure, nervous, judgemental – and loving, giggly, warm, joyous and proud. She's been in the merchant navy, and I can't board a pedalo without worrying that I'll fall in the water. She's travelled all seven seas, when most people can't even name three seas. She's changed the way I think about motherhood, and becoming a mum has somehow made her even more like herself. Fierce, funny and obsessively worrisome.

Beth Facts

⊕ I once spent approximately £40 on a tin of chocolates in a Swiss airport, as a gift for Beth, because the Pierrot doll that had been embossed on the tin lid looked like Klaus Nomi. This is because Beth does such an energetic and compelling rendition of 'Lightnin' Strikes' that Klaus, in his costume, is my mental emblem for her. Whenever I am not with her, I assume she is raising her hands above her head, shrieking, 'I CAN'T STOP! I CAN'T STOP MYSELF!' Even though she lives in Staffordshire with her husband and infant child, and her schedule doesn't really allow it.

✪ Beth and I both took part in the same Brownie talent show, when we were respectively nine and ten. I wore a borrowed wrap dress, persuaded a parent to scrape my hair into an unforgiving chignon, and William Shatnered my way through 'Don't Cry for Me Argentina'. Beth wore a bin bag cloak decorated with tin foil stars and performed a trick she called 'The Clever Banana'.

✪ Beth isn't even called Beth. I call her this, because her Facebook picture and persona is borrowed from Beth Davenport, the character played by Gretchen Corbett in *The Rockford Files.* Beth believes, I think, that having any kind of public persona is slightly more vulgar than shitting inside someone else's recycling box, on bin day.

✪ One day, Beth plans to patent a wart removal cream, called 'Thwart'.

✪ Beth makes very delicious Caipirinhas.

✪ While I would argue that Beth is the most sexually puritanical and Calvinistic of all my sisters, she is supremely skilled at buying presents of beautiful underwear.

✪ As a teenager, Beth wrote several very funny *Simpsons* scripts, which I remember so vividly I sometimes wonder why they're never on TV.

✪ For a long time, Beth was the custodian of a seven-foot mannequin called 'Madam'. Beth bought Madam on Ebay, collected her from Ealing and carried her on the 65 bus, with legs under one arm and Madam's torso on her knee. Madam lived with Beth in Bethnal Green, in Southall and in Nunhead. Madam now resides at our parents' house, sometimes wearing an old school uniform and a wig, lingering outside the dining room and terrifying anyone who has popped round to talk to Mum about the flowers. (Beth even brought Madam to my wedding. She planned to make her part of her speech, but it got a bit complicated and Madam remained in a cupboard. 'Still, at least Madam got to see Greenwich; she's not been before,' said Beth, philosophically. Then: 'Well, if she has, she hasn't mentioned it.')

✪ In Clapham, in 2012, I called Beth a cunt and threw a napkin at her because we were having an argument about avocados.

✪ I am sure that Beth will write novels, and win the Booker Prize one day. I don't know whether I will die of pride, or die of murder-suiciding her.

✪ When she was in middle school, Beth wore the same favourite outfit for every non-uniform day. A yellow and orange tie-dye-effect nylon blouse from Tammy Girl, a huge glass medallion on a long black cord, decorated with a yin and yang symbol, and bright blue John Lennon sunglasses that she bought from a stall at Aylesbury market for £2.50. I almost persuaded her to wear the medallion on her wedding day.

✪ Beth eats pickled eggs, for fun. Sometimes she buys them from chip shops, and she doesn't even get any chips.

✪ By some margin, Beth is the sister least fond of drama, theatre, showing off and public displays of anything. But she has a really lovely singing voice.

CHAPTER FIVE

How Do I Look? Like You!

Women, Body Confidence and Human Mirrors

I've just discovered that my phone has a face recognition feature. I can tap a heart and tell it that a particular face is my favourite, and the phone will find every photo that features that face. I tapped the heart button on a picture of Maddy, at our niece's christening. 'Is this a photo of Maddy?' asked my phone, showing me a picture of Dotty at a festival. I rolled my eyes. 'My smartphone is stupid,' I thought, before trying to label a picture of Livvy, and realising that the photograph was actually of me.

I cannot be objective about my sisters' looks. I can only favourite their faces, because they *are* my favourite faces. To me, these are the most beautiful women in the world. Looking at them brings me more joy than spending an hour in the National Portrait Gallery, staring at old pictures of celebrated beauties, or gazing at supermodels while flicking through *Vogue*. I don't think I see them as other people might. Friends notice their full lips, thick hair and flawless skin.

When I think about their beauty, I think of Beth's fierce

grey-gold eyes, and the way they glitter whenever she's about to tell a joke or start an argument. I think of the bones of Grace's face, their classical proportions and the way they invoke a sense of serenity, and how her skin has softened since she became a mother. I look at Livvy, and think about how her face is the opposite, yet identical, and how expressive and reactive she is from her forehead to her chin. I think of Maddy's radiant warmth, how I don't have any photos of her where she isn't smiling, and how it's impossible not to smile back. I think of Dotty's kind velvet eyes, and the way she grimaces slightly when her face is in repose, as if she's permanently trying not to laugh in church.

Then I think of my face. I picture the patch of rough red rosacea that runs from my right ear to my jaw, the heaviness of my chin, and the way it looks like a full moon if it's captured at the wrong angle. I think of my nose, a dumpy equilateral triangle that I've longed to replace with an elegant isosceles one, and the lines in my forehead that I've had since I was old enough to look in mirrors. How I wish I looked more like a beautiful woman and less like the actor John C. Reilly.

You know what? I *do* look like a beautiful woman. I look like five of them. I can't hate my face when it looks so like the faces I adore the most. When I look at my sisters, I don't feel anything but love. (Admittedly, I also occasionally get hit by waves of irritation that become a full-blown tsunami when the sister I'm staring at has nicked my phone charger.) I have to start feeling the love when I look in the mirror.

There are millions of people who don't want women to feel beautiful, because we're much more useful to them when we feel weak, sad and insecure. It's easy to persuade women to spend hundreds of pounds on products to correct non-existent problems you've created. It's easy to keep women out of your boardrooms, off your screens and away from spheres of influence if you tell them that they need to look impossibly perfect in order to be worth listening to. 'Women are the worst when it comes to judging other women!' is a lie I hear constantly, often repeated and never interrogated. Why are we the worst? Were we born bitchy? Was there a meeting where everyone agreed that our experience of womanhood would be enhanced with a regime of constant starving, shaming, and circling pictures of celebrity cellulite with green Biro, and I wasn't there to object because I was desperate for a wee and struggling with the tiny keypad lock on the loos in Pret?

I believe some women are horrible about the way that other women look because they think it's the way to get on the winning team. Internalised misogyny is simply a playground survival technique. Women are bullied about their bodies constantly, and it's natural to side with the bullies for the sake of safety. This might be why women criticise their own appearance the most. Show me a bitchy woman who watches *TOWIE* purely to slag off the cast's skirt lengths and fake tan choices, and I'll show you a woman who is constantly tuned in to an internal monologue of acidic cruelty. Mirror, mirror, on the wall, I'm going to make myself feel small.

When we're battling our bodies, we're at war with other women. Every flaw we zero in on, every time we torture ourselves for not being slimmer, or bustier, every time we see a chipped nail as evidence of our lack of professional polish, we're hurting every woman who isn't completely perfect – which is every woman in the world. We've united against ourselves to raise beauty standards to a point that stretches beyond the horizon. Ulysses longed to follow knowledge like a sinking star. Sometimes I think I'm pursuing a Barbie body like a sagging arse. If I let myself make it a priority, I could die trying to be perfect according to society's standards, with my goal becoming harder to reach with every year that passes. I'm trying to remember that every time I think my face and body are not good enough, I'm saying that my sisters' faces and bodies – and every other woman's – aren't good enough, either.

Yet when I admire the beauty of my sisters, I can acknowledge and respect my own. Instead of feeling conceited or arrogant (which we all know is the very *worst* thing a woman can be – we're less judgemental of women who commit acts of genocide than women who say that they're really good at handling guns), feeling beautiful makes me kinder. The more beauty I recognise, the more I see around me, and the less threatened I feel by it. We all need to celebrate our own gorgeousness, for the sake of the global sisterhood. We need to make each other feel that we're attractive enough to sit on any chair, stage or panel, and that every single one of us is worth looking at and listening to. Sadly, I don't think the way we look will ever stop mattering. We need to realise that when we feed our anxieties and insecurities, we're helping to grow a beast that is constantly on the rampage, trying to keep us out of our own spaces.

In some lights, I look nothing like my sisters, and in others, I can't pick myself out of the line-up. Similarly, no two women are completely alike, but there are moments when we mirror each other absolutely. We might be strangers but the femininity of our faces and bodies makes us kin. We have a responsibility to look around and like what we see, to recognise spiritual sisterhood. It's imperative that we look inward and outward with great kindness.

CHAPTER SIX
Too Many Feelings

Sometimes, I think I have too many feelings. I giggle and weep with alacrity, and all of my sisters are exactly the same. We are not known for our stoicism. While we're not always kind to each other about our shared vulnerability, we are a family of overreactors.

The first time that Beth and I were united by a common sadness was when the *Jem and the Holograms* video had to go back to the video shop. *Jem* was a late eighties cartoon about an eponymous pop star with pink hair, and the second I laid eyes on her I stopped trying to force any kind of gender binary on poor *Vicky the Viking*. In fact, I stopped caring about anything but Jem, where her magic earrings came from, and how I could join her band, the Holograms. I suspect the real reason that Blockbusters went out of business is that millennials were the first to grow up with the earliest version of entertainment on demand. We never knew a time when having a fourth channel was exciting, or when watching a Hollywood blockbuster of your choosing, in your home, was a novelty and a luxury. We grew up with videos and to us, it was *inconceivable* that you might watch a film, love that film with your whole heart, and then take it back to the shop where any other idiot could bring it into their home and fail

to love it properly, or worse, try to love it as much as you. Or
– and this would be the ultimate horror – they could fail to
rewind it after they finished watching it.

Jem started a revolution in our heads, and we watched
and rewatched it up until the moment that Dad ejected the
cassette and said it was time to take it back to the shop.
Initially, we thought he was joking. Then we wept all day. We
lay, prone, sobbing, screaming and rocking, a reaction that
would only just about be appropriate if we'd watched Dad's
car explode with him in it on the way to the video shop. I
cried into the carpet, shifting positions at intervals when the
fabric became saturated with my distress, and started to
prickle my cheeks. Jem was our truly outrageous new best
friend, and now she was being ripped from our bosom. She
had given us a glimpse of the sort of girls we wanted to be.
Without her, how could we fail to get lost?

The best thing about Jem was that she proved that girls
like us – mousy, overeager, fairly sweet, well behaved and
prone to bursting into tears if we saw a big dog on the other
side of the street – could transform ourselves into fearless
firebrands. Jem was the alter ego of Jerrica Benton, and she
was the practical, hard-working manager of Starlight Music,
until she touched her special earrings and was transformed
into a pink-haired siren with the help of a magical computer,
Synergy. Jem was our proto-Bowie. She gave us hope. She
made us believe in a future in which we could put on our
best dresses – Technicolor tartan, white satin sashes – and go
on a family outing without one of us accidentally falling in
some horse poo while the other one wept in sympathy. Jem
didn't lock herself in the downstairs loo for hours at a time

because she was shy of the gas man. Jem could even have conversations with her sister, Kimber, that didn't end in tears and biting.

Eventually, I got over Jem – or rather, eventually our long-suffering father managed to track down a VHS copy of the cartoon series for home use – but my sisters and I never managed to thicken our skins. We saw tragedy and disaster everywhere we looked. I once cried with noisy shame in the middle of Brownies because I didn't realise that the chocolates we were making were to sell at a Christmas fair, and I'd been telling a baffled Brown Owl how much I was looking forward to eating them. Brown Owl thought I was disproportionately upset because I wasn't getting any chocolate and gave me a fluffy Polo she found at the bottom of her handbag. I didn't know how to tell her that I was just really embarrassed about getting it wrong, so I ate the Polo, even though it definitely had sand on it.

Shortly afterwards, I tried to watch a musical about Mr Men while sitting next to Grace. The curtain went up, and Grace screamed 'MONSTERS!' and cried loudly for the next forty-five minutes. I missed the whole thing. Grace famously cried during a parents evening, when her form teacher told our parents that Grace was one of the most gifted students she had ever taught. 'I just didn't know what else to do with my face!' she explained afterwards. Livvy weeps through her menstrual cramps and swears it's her preferred form of pain relief. Mum took Maddy and Dotty to the cinema to watch *Inside Out*, and likened the experience to attending a wake. 'At one point I got up to go to the loo, came back and noticed that they were in exactly the same position, but in the time it took me to have a wee, the pile of tissues between them had doubled.' Their sensitivity doesn't always need an emotional stimulus – the twins also once simultaneously burst into tears after Beth farted in the car.

Of course, this sort of sensitivity is not unique to my sisters and me. One of my very best friends, who would prefer not to be named, once spent 30p in order to go and have a cry in the King's Cross station toilets because the nearest branch of Leon had run out of the kind of cookie she had been planning to treat herself to all morning. Another friend cried because she was embarrassed about accidentally picking up someone else's deodorant at the gym. When I worked in an office where I was extremely unhappy, I would often hear other women sobbing softly in the toilet cubicles while I dried my eyes and tried to get my breath back. When you've been trying to be tough for hours on end, sometimes the lack of a cookie is what causes you to crumble. When we're taught to take up as little space as possible, invading another woman's space, even accidentally, can be a cause of humiliation. For women, the world is a place where we're often made to feel vulnerable, and then shamed for our vulnerability.

However, we're not sensitive to each other's sensitivity, or rather, we're not above using it as a means of torture. My sisters were especially creative when it came to inventing games to see who could make each other cry first. Their favourite was conceived by the back door, while we were all waiting to get into the car and go to school. Livvy picked up a small bay branch that Mum had brought in from the garden, that was being slowly stripped of its leaves. It was December, possibly the most sentimental of all the months. 'Heartlessly, Mum has *stolen* these bay leaves from some orphans,' she began. 'They don't have any money at the orphanage, and they cannot afford a Christmas tree. So they came into the garden, their ragged clothes being torn by the barren branches, their bones jutting out from underneath, because they are too poor to afford food. But they love each other, and they just want to be together, on Christmas Day, singing carols, gathered around their paltry Christmas twig . . .'

To this day, any of my sisters need only glance at a rapidly shedding plant and mutter something about 'poor orphans' and my face instantly becomes slick with salt water. The only thing that makes me feel slightly better about the imaginary orphans is that the Mitford sisters played exactly the same trick on each other, a ritual immortalised by Nancy in *The Pursuit of Love* with a poem about a 'little houseless match' that should come with a trigger warning. There is a strange safety in crying over things that have been invented expressly for that purpose. You can experience emotional release in a vacuum. Especially when the tears are triggered by someone you love. Strangely, I actually enjoy crying over a story that Livvy has made up, because it's utterly luxurious when I compare it with the alternative – that she makes me cry because she is hurt or in danger. For us, I think that teasing each other to tears gives us a space to experience our sensitivity in the same way that some people love scaring themselves with horror films. You can push yourself to the very brink of your boundaries and then pull back at the last minute, knowing reality is calmer, kinder and safer than the simulated sadness you have chosen to subject yourself to.

Unlike us, my parents did not cry for fun. I have only ever seen Mum cry once, and that was when she caught her hand in a car door. When Princess Diana died, I lied to my school friends. 'My mum cried too; she was really sad,' I boasted, even though Mum was not a fan and only ever referred to her through pursed lips as 'The Princess of Wales', while narrowing her eyes. Diana was One of Us – a weeper, an expresser, a person who seemed to struggle with too many feelings. I'm not sure if this polarised her critics and supporters globally, but it certainly did in our house. While I'm not sure that I could describe my parents as royalists, I think that any positive feelings they had about the Queen were connected with their core belief that HRH would carry on smiling politely and asking people if they'd had far to come even if the corgis leapt on top of her hat and started eating her face.

There is an odd gap between the borderline emotional incontinence of my sisters and me, and the extreme restraint of my parents. I think that either one of them would rather have a stranger take them aside and tell them that they have BO than to be labelled 'emotional' – yet the sadness of their children can be lavish, voluble and indiscriminate, provoked by death, injustice and someone else eating the last Müller Corner.

Dianadeath, as it was christened by the author Helen Fielding, made me aware of the great gulf that lies between the Sensitive and the Tough. Mum and Dad were, I think, both mildly horrified by the televised queues of weeping people paying tribute. I don't think this was due to any heartlessness or a lack of compassion on their part – but perhaps it was the result of a characteristic common to many members of their generation. They were brought up by people who had known tragedy on a scale so grand and absolutely incomprehensible that if you started crying over your loss and pain, you might never, ever stop. Mum and Dad both had fathers who fought in a war. Presumably, when you come home from war, you feel as though you've forfeited the right to be visibly upset by anything ever again. You've known and survived the greatest horror, and you're lucky. To show distress isn't just weak, it's an act of ingratitude. I think my parents both grew up in houses of great stoicism.

So how did they produce six weepy, leaky daughters?

Strangely, I think that our hypersensitivity is a form of strength. We know that life can be gorgeous and awful, and if you're an overreactor, you're built to bend in the wind. If you're constantly holding yourself rigid, determined to be neither visibly devastated, nor pleased, you're too brittle to be flexible and you'll snap. As sisters, and young women, we all swayed in the breeze together. I think we've all been guilty of embracing a reductive stereotype. We're soppy girls! We're the damp gender! We're supposed to have a weekly weep! Don't mind me, it's just that I saw a picture of the footballer Wayne Bridge and that reminded me of bridges, which made me think of *It's A Wonderful Life* and . . . gosh, have you got a tissue? Still, together, we found the stereotype bought us space. No one wants to be branded as emotionally incontinent and then dismissed, but it's much better than the alternative, which is to be told that you're valued because you don't show emotion and made to feel that you're letting everyone down if you fail to suppress a single lip wobble.

Too Many Feelings

As I've got older, I've appreciated the sensitivity of women more than ever. I'm so lucky to be surrounded by strength, in that so many of the women I know are inspiring, ass-kicking, name-taking, self-starting powerhouses of determination, ambition and focus. Yet when these amazing women show me their three-dimensional humanity, and open up about the emotional issues that they struggle to overcome, I feel much more connected to them. We're all under so much pressure to present a perfect front, and we can't afford to have our vulnerabilities exploited. It's an honour when a woman trusts you enough to tell you that she feels as though she failed at an emotional feat of strength. Because we all feel as though we're failing, sometimes. One friend has set up her own hugely successful business, but I didn't realise how hard she was working until she told me that she usually cries once a week about a bad meeting. In her beautiful memoir *The Art of Not Falling Apart,* the journalist Christina Patterson writes a compelling account of the emotional struggles that ensued after she lost her job. It becomes clear that the loss affected her so deeply because she's extremely talented and highly conscientious. Our sensitivity is an expression of deep passion. It isn't a sign of weakness; it's pure fire.

Maddy seems to have an especially evolved emotional metabolism. She forecasts her emotions across her whole face, warning us all of stormy or sunny weather. Although she can be quick to gloom, she rarely stays unhappy for long because she's so good at identifying her feelings and asking for what she needs. Some people believe that we all have an EQ, as well as an IQ, and that our emotional intelligence can be measured by our ability to recognise our own emotions as well as others, and to use that information to behave empathetically and appropriately. I've learned so much from Maddy about using my EQ.

Some years ago, Maddy had her heart pulverised by an especially bad boyfriend. To the casual observer, Maddy's acute distress was a mystery. He was an idiot with unnecessarily complicated hair, with a wardrobe that was like a testament to terrible life choices and the fact that he lived not that far away from a branch of TK Maxx. Maddy is a human 1948 Ford Deluxe, the car that Danny Zuko flies into the sky at the very end of *Grease*. This boy was a traffic warden's wheel clamp. Most people expected Maddy to weep for half an hour and then jump up and sing 'I Will Survive', while shaking maracas. But she was sad for weeks. Yet the more she expressed her sadness, the better she became at separating herself from her feelings. As she described how betrayed and hurt she felt, she found a way to grieve the relationship, while understanding why it had to end. Maddy made me realise how strange it is that we talk about surviving our feelings by 'putting on a brave face'. Because it's much, much braver to embrace your unhappiness, and be open and honest about your vulnerability. It's like stretching a muscle. Being open to sadness keeps you emotionally supple, but staying taut and rigid can only lead to cramp.

Maddy is my Roy Walker of mental health. She encourages me to say what I see ('Flames! World ending!). I don't think I'd be here writing this if it weren't for her. I'd be sobbing into my sleeve, or obsessively checking that my house keys were in my bag for the ninth time this minute. Maddy especially made it OK for me to say, 'I'm not OK.' Also, she made me realise that as her big sister, she didn't need me to be perfect, and inspire her by never revealing a single flaw. She showed me that I'm much more useful to her, and our other sisters, if I talk openly about the times when I'm sad or scared. Our emotions are only a problem if we feel isolated by them.

In books and movies, it has become fashionable to talk about the importance of 'strong female characters'. In lots of ways, this is admirable. It means that women see women who are three-dimensional, consistent and have authentic voices – rather than women who turn up at the end and say, 'Together we've saved America from the intergalactic aliens with machine guns. Now save me with your underpants gun.' The trouble is that the 'strong woman' is becoming a reductive stereotype too. A 'strong woman' on screen is a woman in a skirt suit who can earn a billion dollars a minute while taking seven phone calls, then lets a single tear roll down her face, illuminated by the light of the microwave, while she waits for her 'I have no personal life' lasagne. Or a woman who rescues her kidnapped daughter from an underground cave, wearing nothing but a harness, while making sure her facial expression never rises above a level of distress that can be surmised as 'How can Yodel have left a "Sorry you were out" card when I've been sitting on my doormat for six hours?'

When we talk about strength, we're using an old-fashioned, masculine measure. It doesn't serve anyone. When we praise women for their strength, we're usually congratulating them for not being so darn annoyingly female! The patriarchy loves it when women don't show their feelings, because they usually cause great inconvenience. Sadness especially can rarely be practically fixed, or explained away, so for thousands of years, men have been telling everyone – not just women – to do the next best thing and ignore feelings as much as possible. Mum has four big brothers, and I wonder whether that's connected with her reluctance to weep. She was raised in a house filled with men, during an era in which the worst thing anyone could be accused of was 'soppiness'.

It's interesting that 'snowflake' has become the ultimate term of abuse – and it's typically used to draw a line between the old and the young, as well as, more often than not, the dry-eyed and the weeper. When people criticise snowflakes, they're expressing fury. Like generations before them, they had to endure their troubles silently, so why can't we? We've ended up with a situation in which the person with the highest emotional pain threshold gets to set the bar, and everyone suffers and struggles as a result. When we try to be tough, no one wins. When we're vulnerable together, we learn from each other, and we're able to appeal to everyone's better nature. It's deeply humanising.

However, I think we live in an emotional period. Sadness is starting to lose a little bit of its stigma. Together, my sisters and I have been training to match the mood of the age! Admittedly, some sadness is a sign of extreme self-involvement. I admit that I feel an abstracted sort of misery in response to a humanitarian disaster, and a different, venal, urgent kind when my jeans won't do up. Still, largely, I think that most millennials are significantly more compassionate than the generations that have preceded us, and this is because we're used to understanding and connecting with each other's pain. When you're extremely sensitive, you're very aware of other people's feelings. When my sisters and I aren't trying to make each other cry, we're very kind to each other, because we know how it feels to be extremely sensitive in a world that wants you to be tough. Together, we build homes for each other, spaces to be sensitive, where we can fall apart and put each other back together.

CHAPTER SEVEN

King Lear, Cinderella and Me

Big sisters come off quite badly in most works of literature. We're venal, egotistical, grasping, manipulative and rough. Little sisters are vulnerable, elegant and noble. They are adept at self-sacrifice. They have a charisma and charm that shines through and enchants everyone they meet, even when they're bent over a bucket with a scrubbing brush, up to their elbows in horse shit. Even the better big sisters are boring, compared with their sexier, sparkier siblings. There's Jane in *Pride and Prejudice*. Dull as fuck. There's Meg in *Little Women*. Lazy, bossy and easily led. There's Rose Mortmain in *I Capture the Castle* – an indecisive, self-absorbed homewrecker who will sell out her friends and family for a nice new nightie. There's Goneril and Regan from *King Lear*, who are so awful that they inspired my father's favourite expression of brattiness: 'How sharper than a serpent's tooth it is to have a thankless child!' Then there are the Ugly Sisters.

The Ugly Sisters are so loathed that they are not even named (although in Disney's version, they go by Anastasia and Drusilla). Their 'ugliness' is subjective – in the film, they have misshapen noses, unflattering fringes and a penchant for outsize hair accessories. They're trapped in a vicious circle.

They are cruel to Cinderella because they are jealous of her beauty. This unkindness somehow manifests itself physically, making the sisters appear even uglier. Which exacerbates their jealousy, and meanness. The Ugly Sisters never had a chance. They served one function – to enhance Cinderella's established beauty and good character. They are one-dimensional and disposable. And we're meant to laugh at them. We're meant to be indignant that either sister believed she could ever stand a chance with the prince, and that they're not just ugly, but vain and delusional about it.

Everything is wrong with *Cinderella*. It's a story that punishes women with ambition, and makes us believe that the best way to get ahead is with good behaviour, and respecting curfews. Its central message makes me certain that the Brothers Grimm were in that creepy category of men who fetishise natural beauty and think it's OK to slutshame women for wearing false eyelashes. Most upsettingly, as a UK size nine who can only really wear Clarks and Converse, it suggests that you're an unfeminine freak if you're a woman with big feet. If I'd dashed down the palace steps and lost a crystal slipper, a servant would have picked it up, assuming that someone was trying to nick one of the prince's gravy boats.

We think that Cinderella is a story about a reversal of fortunes, but it's a story that pits women against women – sisters against sisters. We're led to believe that the wicked stepmother encourages her daughters to scheme against Cinderella. We don't think about the circumstances that led to these strange relationships, or even about the relationship between the Ugly Sisters themselves. We share this story with children without wondering how they will relate to it, and what it's like to assume that you're too bossy and bigfooted to ever be Cinderella – so you *must* be an Ugly Sister. It becomes prophetic, and you become ashamed of your efforts to be beautiful and good, knowing they're inadequate.

Real-life sister stories are complex, nuanced and layered, but fictional sisters tend to get one-word descriptors, brief sketches and storylines. When I was little, we were endlessly compared to the Bennet girls in *Pride and Prejudice*, and I remember feeling desperately sorry for poor Mary – nerdy, obnoxious, and not nearly as clever as she thinks she is – and Kitty, whose sole function seems to be following Lydia around and giggling like an idiot. Jane Austen's other depictions of sisters seem much more real – Elinor Dashwood in *Sense and Sensibility* is a rare big sister who gets to be sparky and self-sacrificing, and you don't need to be the baby of the bunch to identify with her dreamier, more impulsive sister Marianne. But it's hard to read stories where sisters are reduced to bit parts, canvases to colour and contrast with the adventures of the heroine, when I feel as though my sisters *are* my story.

The myth that women instinctively fail to support other women is exacerbated by the way that sisters are portrayed in books. Admittedly if everyone got on and adored each other, you'd end up with an extremely boring story, but sisters are often used as vehicles for tension and envy. Even my favourites, the Dashwood girls, struggle to pass the Bechdel test – they might be more kind and supportive of each other than most, but they're focused on the pursuit of Colonel Brandon and Edward Ferrars.

Of course, one of the biggest struggles of sisterhood is working out how to share a spotlight. In *Cinderella*, the heroine seems to win it by not wanting it, and the Ugly Sisters are left out in the cold because they visibly long to be centre stage. When I think of them now, I think of their vulnerability, and the cruelty of the fact that they're so conspicuous, but never really seen. Sometimes I think that I have a serious Ugly Sister complex, and at times, all of my little sisters have been Cinderella-style vampires – knowing it's very easy to look good as long as I look bad. And I never felt more like Cinderella than I did when Beth punched me on the bus.

If we had been brothers, the story would have seemed very different. We'd just be a pair of little lads having a scrap and getting carried away. But when Beth punched me – and I can't remember what I said to make her do it, but I am certain I deserved it – I felt feminine for the first time. I wasn't a thundering, lumpen oaf, but a little bird with a broken wing, delicate enough to hurt, instead of being the sturdy girl who was always being told to be careful with her sisters, because she 'didn't know her own strength'.

We're told that Cinderella never responds to her sisters' taunts and acts of cruelty, simply simpering and choosing to rise above them. By being passive and not complaining, she was rewarded. I think it would be a better story if Cinderella had hit back, metaphorically and literally. We need to see her humanity and her sisters' vulnerability. If they'd have fought fiercely, made it up and hugged it out, they could have all gone to the ball together, cleaned the palace out of prosecco and ignored the drippy prince and his shoe fetish.

Without wishing to encourage violence, I wish that we could read stories in which sisters are allowed to fight, disagree and want things. I wish that fairy tales didn't celebrate so many silent women, and a little part of me wishes that, instead of feeling smug and sanctimonious, revelling in my saint-like status, I had punched Beth back.

King Lear has some similarities to *Cinderella*. You have two bad sisters who are up against one good one. You also see the consequences of parental favouritism. Cinderella's stepmother encourages her daughters to ostracise and torment the heroine. Lear divides his kingdom unequally among his daughters, offering the biggest share to the child who professes to love him the most. He splits it between Goneril and Regan, leaving out Cordelia, who refuses to flatter him with false hyperbole. Goneril is a villain, prepared to say anything to her father in order to promote her succession, and Regan is playing by the same rules. Spoiler alert – Goneril and Regan both end up fighting over Edmund, and Goneril poisons her sister before killing herself. We're supposed to think these women are selfish monsters. We're not invited to consider the fact that when sisters are ugly or evil, there is usually a manipulative parent hovering.

If you're the favourite, you're probably the villain, and it's not always clear whether a parent is using their power of preference to play you off against your siblings, or whether becoming the favourite is a means to an end in the pursuit of power.

In 2005, a study of 384 families* found that 74 per cent of mothers and 70 per cent of fathers would give preferential treatment to a particular child. Also, the research found that more often than not, the first borns were the ones who felt

---

* https://www.ncbi.nlm.nih.gov/pubmed/16402879

that they were the preferred sibling. Lead researcher Katherine Conger explained: 'Our working hypothesis was that older, earlier born children would be more affected by perceptions of differential treatment due to their status as older child – more power due to age and size, more time with parents – in the family.' But it's rare that anyone feels like the favourite. We only notice when someone else seems to be getting more love or attention. Conger adds: 'Everyone feels their brother or sister is getting a better deal.'

In 2018, Alisha Tierney-March, the mother of three girls and a boy, enraged viewers of *This Morning* by going on the programme to say that she believes every mother has a favourite child, and hers is her two-year-old daughter Kennedie. Many people commented on the fact that her admission would damage and hurt her other children. I would be horrified if my mother had been on national television and told millions of viewers that she loved Beth best, or that Maddy was the child she felt the most connected to. Equally, I think I'd be horrified if she picked me. But I think that it must be impossible for parents to feel equally bonded to their children at all times – just as it sometimes feels impossible for us to make sense of our parents' relationships with our siblings.

I don't believe my parents have ever displayed any overt favouritism, but that's never stopped us from accusing them of having a favourite or even from trying to win the title. This is accompanied by the strange and occasionally cruel impulse to celebrate when a sister is in trouble – after all, if they've done something wrong and are getting shouted at, you're probably in the clear. If someone else is being bollocked for failing to finish their carrots, you can gain points by drawing attention to the fact that you have eaten all of yours.

Favouritism holds us back, even when it's a concept that only exists in our heads. Being in any group makes me deeply anxious, because I feel as though I have so little control of the group dynamic. It's difficult to resist the urge to fight for favour, and concentrate on just being, instead of being the most liked. All groups are like little families, and the favourites aren't necessarily the ones with the best grades and clean plates. When I managed groups of interns at the teen magazine *Bliss*, I was jokingly referred to as the 'mum', and my favourite interns weren't the best writers or most proficient journalists, but the ones who reminded me of me. The earnest, awkward girls who were extremely clever and slightly too shy to show it. The quietly goofy ones, who seemed serious until they slowly revealed a penchant for extreme silliness. Unfairly, I was prejudiced against the most confident, glamorous girls, because of my own insecurities and fears.

Obviously supervising some interns cannot be compared with a lifetime of parenting, but my relationship with these girls has led me to reflect on my relationship with my mother. When I felt the most jealous of my sisters, especially Beth and Grace, it was because they seemed so similar to Mum, and much closer to her for that reason. Mum is elegant, gamine, carelessly chic, and has a moral horror of vanity. To put it mildly, I think she was quite surprised to give birth to a daughter who seemed to have less in common with her than with RuPaul and Danny La Rue. In many ways, Mum's attitude was revelatory. My friends' mothers talked about cellulite and Lean Cuisine, but I don't think Mum has ever cared or known what she weighs. I don't really remember her looking in the mirror, apart from to check for smudges after lighting the coal fire.

I lived for pink. I craved the girly, sparkly and hyperfeminine, and Mum didn't even have a tube of lipstick I could play with. Beth and Grace seemed less concerned about pretty dresses and performance. They were happy to roll around in the mud, and didn't burst into tears and sulk for an hour if someone tried to persuade them to wear a blue jumper. I think Mum was genuinely scared that her first born was going to grow into the sort of woman she had been to school with, and would jump into a bush to avoid on the street – the kind that drives a custom-sprayed pink Fiat 500 with a sticker on the back that reads 'My other car is a unicorn'.

I wanted Mum to be like me, and I felt as though I'd let her down badly by being less like her. I could not get her to back my plan to write to Jimmy Saville and ask him to fix it for me to have all of my Barbies' clothes made in my size. (Obviously, we both now agree that this was a great act of foresight on her part.)

Looking back, I think we were just both executing tiny rebellions. Mum did not want her life to be defined by the expectation that she should look or behave a certain way, as a woman. She was extremely busy looking after a family, and there was no way that she was going to waste time or money to fulfil someone else's arbitrary standard. More importantly, she was a child of the sixties and seventies. Make-up was for *her* mum. It belonged to an era when you couldn't go out on a weekday morning without wearing a hat, and people would die of indigestion before they stopped wearing a girdle. I

93

lusted for glamour, and I'd compare Mum to her sister-in-law, Auntie Maria, who had blonde hair, like mine, and wore blue eyeshadow, which I was forbidden from doing.

At the time, toys seemed incredibly gendered. I dreamed about Barbies, Sindy's make-up counter that came with real perfume, and Girl's World, the plastic bust that allowed its owners to pretend they were hairdressers, a job that was always in my top five of future employment options. Everything that had alienated and restricted my mother seemed aspirational to me, yet my girliness made me feel like a family outcast.

The film *Lady Bird* features an exchange between the main character and her mother that is, I think, a startlingly perfect summation of how it feels to know you'll never be the favourite, though it's all you long for, even if it's only for a moment.

'I just wish . . . I wish that you liked me,' says Lady Bird, as she tries on discount prom dresses and struggles with her mother's hypercritical comments. Her mum, Marion, immediately replies that she *loves* her. 'But do you *like* me?' pleads Lady Bird. I felt viscerally shocked, drained of oxygen, to see the actor Saoirse Ronan, looking like a princess, playing a character who admits to neediness and vulnerability, who doesn't feel special or liked or beloved. The film is about her mother, not her siblings, but she is still made to feel selfish, flawed and manipulative, like an Ugly Sister. She doesn't get to be Cinderella.

Mum says it took her some time to understand and appreciate the ways in which I wasn't like her – but when she did, she started to appreciate the differences between all her daughters. Because I was the first, the difference was a shock, but by the time Maddy and Dotty arrived she was so used to the ways in which we varied that the similarities astonished her.

However, now that I'm in my thirties, I think I'm more like my mum than I ever realised. Occasionally my husband is shocked by our striking similarities, when we're together – the way we speak at the same pitch and cadence, using the same expressions. The way we'll stick our elbows out at identical angles to top up each other's wineglasses, the way we both laugh from our bellies at the same stupid puns. As soon as I stopped worrying about the fact that I wasn't the daughter she wanted, and my sisters were, we became closer and started to understand each other better.

Also, I think Mum is the missing link between my sisters and me. In Beth, I see Mum's originality, her refusal to follow the crowd without asking questions first. In Grace, her kindness, and her drive to make sure everyone is safe, happy and comfortable. Livvy has her sociable streak, her ability to speak to anyone at a party. Maddy shares her instinctive understanding of psychology, and her curiosity about why we do what we do. And Dotty has her power and stillness, her ability to command respect and attention without demanding it. We're reflections of her, and as we get older we distort and subvert the light, taking her essence and creating new, original pictures of her own. I think that we all felt like Ugly Sisters, growing up. But now, when we're together, we are all swans. I don't feel defined by my bossiness, by my sisters' vulnerability or my ranking. I'm simply a sister, a daughter, a woman and a friend.

The Best Books About Sisters

The Pursuit of Love by Nancy Mitford
Narrator Fanny and heroine Linda are really cousins, not
sisters, but their shared obsessions, fights, fears and
suffocating intimacies make them siblings - biology is
immaterial.

Ballet Shoes by Noel Streatfield
Pauline, Petrova and Posy are orphans adopted and brought
up together during the Second World War. Again, this is a
story about sisterhood that goes beyond biology, and about
loving your similarities and being thrilled by your differences.

Little Fires Everywhere by Celeste Ng
This utterly compelling book features one of my favourite
sisterly relationships in literature - between Lexie, the eldest
Richardson daughter, and Pearl, who with her mother is
lodging in the family's second home. You don't have to be
someone's birth sister to be the sister they need when they're
going through a crisis.

Pride and Prejudice by Jane Austen
This is considered by most readers to be the textbook on
sisterhood. Austen draws the symbiotic ecosystem of a family
with startling vividness and veracity.

Sisterland by Curtis Sittenfeld
Identical twins Kate and Violet have ESP (extrasensory
perception), but Kate is determined to bury her powers while
Violet seeks to exploit them. Sittenfeld is excellent on love,
conflict and the detail of domestic life.

The Favourite Sister by Jessica Knoll
A contemporary story about how even adult sisters struggle

to share a spotlight. Knoll writes about success, envy and competition between sisters with wit and startling accuracy.

Watermelon (and the other Walsh Girls books) by Marian Keyes
The Walsh sisters – Claire, Rachel, Maggie, Anna and Helen – have been my fictional friends since my teens. Every woman has a story to tell and Keyes captures the kindness, claustrophobia, animosity and love of family life with a level of detail so keen that I've wondered whether she's spying on me. The Walshes are the fictional family most like my own.

Man at the Helm by Nina Stibbe
Stibbe is one of the greatest comic writers I've ever read. The story of nine-year-old Lizzie Vogel working with her big sister to try to find her mother a boyfriend is hilarious and tragic in turns, but for me the most special part of Stibbe's novel is the way she captures the practical telepathy that develops between siblings and the rhythms of language shared.

The Water Cure by Sophie Mackintosh
An eerie, unworldly exploration about how sisters seek to love, protect and hurt each other in a dystopian world where men have become toxic to women.

Little Women by Louisa May Alcott
One of the things I love the most about this book is that I believe every one of us can relate to all of the March girls within the same day – it's a story about women reconciling who they are with who they believe they ought to be. (If ever there was a proto *Gone Girl* Cool Girl, it was Jo March.)

Beezus and Ramona by Beverly Clearly
Beezus (really Beatrice, rechristened by her little sister) is the responsible, frequently frustrated nine-year-old who is driven to distraction by her little sister – everyone finds Ramona adorable, and when she isn't, it's Beezus' fault. This is the bible for big sisters, whether you're nine or forty-nine.

The Star Side of Bird Hill by Naomi Jackson
When it's decided that their mother can no longer care for them, sixteen-year-old Dionne and ten-year-old Phaedra are sent away from their home in Brooklyn to live with their grandmother in Barbados, in the summer of 1989. This is a heartbreaking and beautiful novel about sisters seeing themselves in each other during the transition between girlhood and womanhood, and the most joyful and painful elements of being part of a family.

CHAPTER EIGHT

The Christmas Chapter

Perhaps the best way to explain how my family functions is to tell you about Christmas.

My dad *adores* Christmas. My mum regularly makes a joke about Dad that perhaps only eight people in the world – us – find funny. It's her riff on St Augustine's 'We are an Easter people, and "Alleluia" is our song'. She says, of my father, 'He is a Christmas man, and "Jingle Bells" is his song.'

Dad is indeed a Christmas man. Like Santa, he prepares all year long, gathering gifts, claiming hiding places, making lists and checking them twice, thrice, squinting at bits of paper balanced on piles of packages while standing in line at John Lewis. I still can't decipher my father's handwriting because I taught myself not to look, even though I longed to read my seasonal runes and see what was in store for me. I remember Dad calling my bluff after a trip into town, when I was showing too much interest in the contents of the carrier bags. 'Do you want to know what you're getting? Here, I'll show you!' I ran from the room.

The greatest telling off that I remember getting as a child happened on Christmas Eve Eve, when my sisters and I sneaked into Dad's study and started clawing at packages as if we were playing the bonus round on *Catchphrase*, hoping to guess our gifts by tearing off tiny panels of paper, even though I don't think that we really wanted to know before Christmas morning. During the month of December, we devoted our lives to second guessing Dad's system, but we were all Wile E. Coyotes to his Road Runner. We knew the game was unwinnable and we didn't want victory, for it would have disturbed the order of the universe.

Christmas was when I witnessed my parents' 'love languages' in action. In 1992, an American self-help author named Gary Chapman published a book that suggested there are five main ways of expressing love – giving someone words of affirmation, quality time, gifts, touch or acts of service. The trouble with the system is that it assumes that our instincts will override societal pressures – it doesn't take account of the fact that women especially are expected to constantly perform acts of service, as well as being the ones who are expected to give up their time to look after other people. We can't always choose our love languages freely. We're propelled into acts of service, because that is what has been expected of us for thousands of years. It's only relatively recently that we know our words of affirmation deserve to be listened to, or that we've been able to earn our own money to buy the gifts we want to give. Mum is one of the most thoughtful, kind and empathetic people I know, but I realise that she feels as though she's expected to express that kindness by being the perfect hostess.

When I think of the ways Mum says 'I love you', I can taste the home-made lasagne she'd cook on my first night home for the Christmas holidays, tenderness made deep and crisp and even. I think of how she makes my bed up with

Irish linen, a luxury she longed for during years of early marriage and practical polycotton, a necessity brought about by children and their unreliable bladders. I think of the heft and heaviness of the back door, the push followed by the squeeze as Mum clasps her arms around me and asks about my journey and whether I want a cup of tea or a glass of wine. Mum and Dad both share an ability to show their love selflessly. Their ways of saying 'I love you' make the recipient the subject, not the object. Dad's presents are carefully chosen reflections of the tastes of the person whose name is on the tag, not his. Mum cares about making other people comfortable, rather than impressing them.

Most importantly, my parents share a sixth love language – literature. Everyone knows that the Christmas chapter is the best in any book, and when you have a gaggle of daughters, you've already assembled your cast of characters. If you have a bookish sensibility, impressionable children and a fondness for fairy lights, you can make magic happen with ease.

When we were little, the magic was easy to maintain. If someone kicked a can down the street within my earshot, I was convinced that I'd heard the sound of jingle bells, and that the seasonal Stasi (elves) were checking on our behaviour and reporting back to Santa. But when I was eleven, I was convinced, like the March girls, that Christmas couldn't be Christmas, partly because I was greasy and gross and hormonal, but mostly because I had broken my leg, and I was encased in plaster from left foot to thigh. I felt like crap on crutches, and I couldn't do anything Christmassy because I was so clumsy and immobile. No singing in the choir. No running to the bottom of the garden with my arms outstretched, convinced I had seen snow fall. (It was usually a carrier bag caught in a tree.) No giggly trips to Superdrug on a Saturday spending my pocket money on gifts that cost £1.50 and claimed to smell of musk. I was miserable.

Dad was more concerned about my lack of Christmas spirit than my leg itself. (The Buchanans are proudly sedentary people – and at points I think the rest of the family envied me my enforced spell of stillness.) His eldest daughter was one sulk away from Humbug territory, so he came up with a plan. On 20 December, the feast of St School's Out, or Christmas Eve Eve Eve Eve Eve, he presented my sisters and me with the Festive Programme of Events – a timetable of fun that promised tree decorating, the telling of Christmas ghost stories, quizzes, magical mystery tours and an afternoon dedicated to the writing of thank you letters. (It's the curse of the middle classes. My parents would rather receive a telephone call informing them that one of us was being incarcerated for murder than one from a relative saying that they felt insufficiently thanked for a Body Shop bath pearl set.)

The Programme of Events became as traditional as the 'handwritten' letter from Father Christmas, left next to a smeary sherry glass and a carrot stub. No matter how deeply we had chosen to impale ourselves on the claws of adolescence, we would line up like the Von Trapps to receive our little booklets. Even now, it makes me feel tender and tearful to think of Dad in his office, photocopying and stapling pages decorated with pictures of snowmen he had hand drawn in Pentel ink. Eventually it was phased out as we grew up and started to spend Christmas with our partners' families. Still, new practices took its place. Come to my parents' house for Christmas, and you will be asked to write and read out a ghost story on Christmas Eve, probably under the influence of half a bottle of Stone's Green Ginger Wine.

Sometimes the Programme makes special reappearances – for example, all of the guests were issued with one on our wedding day. (It included a quiz, and a fake 'personal ad' from Dad – 'WANTED: CASH . . . for a father whose daughters keep getting married. All currencies accepted. No Bitcoins.') It was Dad's way of teaching us that Christmas is a time for tradition, but that no one can stop you from making up brand new traditions to go with the old ones. As adults, my sisters and I have started our own – cocktails in Claridge's, and a trip to see the tree, and elaborate Christmas lunches with old friends and housemates in the middle of December, putting the Mariah Carey Christmas album on heavy rotation. These rituals are the legacy of the Programme of Events. Mum and Dad made Christmas feel as fond and familiar as rereading a beloved book. They showed me that it was a time to express love, and that magic happens when you start to realise there are infinite ways of showing it.

The Fairy Dress

Mum might have been baffled by my girly sensibilities, but she did her very best to understand them, and I never felt more understood than when she made me a magical gift.

I've always been ambitious, and the first thing I ever *really* wanted to be was a fairy. Princesses did not have magical powers, air hostesses were made to wear a fairly restrictive uniform, and I had lost interest in running a sweet shop after a lady at Thorntons had explained to me that she was not allowed to eat the stock. To me, fairies were the epitome of all that was pretty and powerful. As far as I could tell, it was a career that was open to all. You didn't need any special qualifications, just the right outfit. I longed for a fairy dress, even though I wasn't absolutely sure what fairies wore.

I'd engage Mum in long conversations about what such a garment might look like, and where I might get it from. 'Would it look like this?' she'd guess, sketching a flower fairy on top of a shopping list, an elegant ballerina with wings and a tulle tutu. 'NO! NOTHING LIKE THAT! It needs to be more . . . sticky-outy,' I'd say, struggling to express myself. Now, I realise Mum was drawing the sort of fairies that Kiera Knightley might play if Richard Curtis wrote his own version of *A Midsummer Night's Dream*. What I wanted, although I couldn't articulate it, was a fairy dress fit for Gemma Collins. Pink on pink, stiff and trembling with glitter, fit for the doll that got to cover Dame Barbara Cartland's bog roll. A dress that went against every single one of my Mum's style sensibilities.

Getting hold of a fairy dress became an issue of deep concern. If I couldn't make Mum understand, how was I going to tell Father Christmas? At the time, Beth's favourite piece of fancy dress kit was a towel. She liked to get out of the bath, wrap it around her shoulders and pretend to be a cat. The origins of this game were a mystery, but at least she could easily access a bath sheet.

The Fairy Dress

I remember it as a period of loneliness and longing. In my head, I was constantly casting spells, but just how magical was I if I couldn't even explain the kind of girl I wanted to be? I was obsessed with transforming myself and escaping my dull, dumpy shell. All I wanted was to be special, and for someone to understand why this mattered.

Mum did her best to distract me, and when fairy dresses were mentioned, she would change the subject. Beth had imaginary kittens. The sticky summer evaporated and soon it was almost the end of autumn, and I was trying to make myself believe that the fog of condensation I saw when I breathed out was a special spirit I had created that would help me in my quest to find Fairyland. Christmas approached, and I was so excited and so scared. What if I got exactly what I wanted, *and what if I didn't?* I couldn't bear the idea that there might not be any magic for me in the world.

There were plenty of presents, but no fairy dress. However, my Nan and Grandpa got me the most gloriously girly of gifts, a bright pink parasol and matching handbag. I paraded around the house with the parasol at full mast, like a Southern belle begging for a spell of bad luck, dragging poor Beth behind me, until Mum suggested that I open some other presents and stop waving the parasol about for the sake of the ocular health of our guests.

It had been such an exciting, distracting day that I'd forgotten about the missing item on my list. Maybe I just wasn't magical enough yet, and Father Christmas would catch me next year. But after lunch, just as the sky darkened and Beth was starting to bunch her fists and rub her eyes, Mum sat down and told us that Father Christmas had left another present for us, but it was too big for our stockings. With Dad, she fetched two huge boxes wrapped in shiny gold paper, one for me and one for Beth.

Opening the lid, I noticed the gleam of pink ribbon, and the curve of something white and tissue-like, edged in glitter. Carefully, I lifted the pink from the box. It was perfect. Everything I had dreamed of and hadn't been able to describe. The straps of the dress were made from wide, blossom-pink ribbon, and adorned with two ruffs of candy pink netting. The rose bodice was smocked and adorned with bows, and it met more netting, which had been gathered into the stickiest-outiest skirt of my dreams. Beth's dress was yellow, and we both had wings and a wand. I *was* magical, and my sister was too.

At the time, I didn't know that Mum had been up every night for months, sewing and sweating, her mouth full of pins and ribbon. I truly believed our perfect dresses had fallen out of the sky. However, now I know that Mum has always loved me and my sisters deeply, dearly and ferociously, even though she hasn't always been able to understand us. That even though she was bewildered by my impulse to twirl myself into a pink blur, she respected it, and she made it matter to her because it mattered to me. She has always treated my sisters and me as though we are made of magic. You can be granted superpowers just as long as someone else wants to see them in you.

CHAPTER NINE

Fierce, Fraught
and Fabulous

The Sisterhood and Female Friendship

Whenever someone learns that I have five sisters, they always respond in the same, specific way. They tilt their head a little to the left, their pupils dilate fractionally and a misty sort of tenderness descends upon them, as if I'm a puppy and they are imagining me engaged in a bout of friendly bum sniffing with a gang of other puppies. 'And are you all *very* close?' they ask. And I am obliged to channel the same mistiness and reply, 'Yeah, we are,' in a way that implies we can leave no strand of each other's hair unbraided. No one ever says, 'Holy shit! I bet that's tough! What's the most violent thing you've ever done to each other? You can tell me, my cousin is in the Marines!' The world expects us to be the very best of friends, for the sake of sweetness, symmetry and convenience.

When you're a girl, or a woman, your womanhood is supposed to be enough common ground to sustain a best friendship. If it isn't, and you clash with each other, or simply fail to connect, you're bitches who are only out for yourselves.

If you can't be friends you must be enemies. People will assume you're defined by a petty rivalry, and they'll judge you for it. As women, our relationships, and the emotional connections behind those relationships are always believed to be binary. There is only love and hate. Not all sisters are close, and it's not because they've fallen out. Sharing a name or a face is no guarantee of friendship, and it's not fair to women to assume that we only have enough imagination to experience one feeling, or its opposite. My friend Eleanor tells me, 'I have two sisters – one is five years older, and one is three years younger, but we're just not that close. Of course I love them, and I'm always happy to see them, but we don't really hang out or spend time together when we're not gathered together for a family occasion. I wish we were best friends; I feel as though we're somehow letting ourselves down by not being good mates. But we're really different, and we can never relax around each other. It's not a bad relationship, it's just an OK one. Yet, even within our own family, there's a myth that we're all really good friends. It's quite exhausting.'

My sisters are my good, dear friends, but that friendship has taken our collective lifetimes to establish – and it's filled with tension and complication. Frankly it would be odd if it *wasn't*. Yet, I feel a lot of pressure for it to be perfect. It's difficult for me to admit that even now, my relationship with my sisters is far from ideal, and sometimes that makes me feel like a failure. Social media makes me feel bad about my body, concerned about my career and worried about my wardrobe, but my biggest source of social anxiety is #squadgoals. The girl gang – the kind that Taylor Swift can assemble within forty-five minutes and position on inflatable pool floats, not the sort that have knives and lurk around unlit alleys – is having a moment. Cool girls grab their best friends together and coo, 'These girls are my *sisters*,' but what are you supposed to do when your sisters aren't your best friends, especially when they inspire a love within you that's fierce, frightening and difficult to corral?

The squad can be limiting. It doesn't always allow space for everyone in the group to exist, or provide an ecosystem that supports separate needs, desires and quirks. Friendship is usually built on common interests, but in theory, a squad requires discrete, complementary personalities in order to function. As a friend and a sister, I've always struggled to find my place within a group because I have a tendency to contort myself to fit the space available, instead of making sure that there really is room for me. It helps to remember that there is a lot of power in stillness, and that you can usually serve your own needs surprisingly well by listening before you speak. Age has taught me to keep the faith too. The first squad you find is inevitably not the right one, but it's probably the one that will rub off your sharp edges. This is good, because if your corners aren't smooth you're going to puncture all of the pool floats.

I believe vulnerability is an important part of friendship, and I'm not good at being vulnerable with my sisters. As the eldest, it's always been my role to protect my girls, to maintain order, and to be there for them when they fall apart. It's only recently that I've made an effort to let my guard down, to ask them for advice and to be honest about my fears and worries. What's worse is that I become very resentful when my sisters protect and help each other. That's *my* job!

Last year, Beth and Grace both gave birth to beautiful babies, within a month of each other. When someone you love dearly and deeply produces a small, adorable, brand new being, you feel as though the new love might kill you. You're *constipated* with it. Holding these tiny babies felt too wonderful to bear. If I were to take a lot of MDMA and then watch *Titanic* I might be able to simulate a tenth of the emotion that I felt when I met Penny and Arthur for the first time. But I was experiencing all of that as an auntie. My job was limited to giddily spending three hundred quid in Baby Boden, and jumping up and down doing an odd approximation of a burpee in order to make the babies laugh. Beth and Grace had experienced something transcendental, and they had done it together. They were on the same life-altering journey at exactly the same time, and they were forging a brand new friendship as adult women. And I felt shut out, frightened and sick with envy. Those horrible feelings were compounded by my certainty that only a really horrible person would be jealous of a pair of happy, pregnant people.

For me, the hardest part was probably that my friendship with Beth had always been tense and tricky, but Gracie was my girl. Beth was, and is, my button pusher. Perhaps because we're so close in age, she has always known exactly how I'm wired, and how those wires might be tripped. However, the slightly bigger age gap between Grace and I means that, for a brief period during my teens, she laboured under the misapprehension that I was cool. As adults, we've established that neither one of us is cool but she has a lingering idea of me as the grown-up girl with the boyfriend who can make strawpedos – even though she now has a husband and a subscription to a wine club.

Grace and I love nothing more than making each other laugh, and Grace has always come to me for advice, mostly on which phone to get, or whether it's worth spending thirty quid on a mascara. Yet, when she realised she was pregnant with her longed-for baby, it was Beth's wisdom she wanted to benefit from, and Beth she wanted to bond with. Together, they giggled over the apps that told them their babies were the size of a tomato, a potato, an endive. 'Yeah, well, my *food baby* is the size of a family pack of Kettle Chips!' I'd say, desperate to join in. They didn't laugh.

However, I started to realise that I didn't need to share the experience to share *in* their experience, and I could be a good friend and sister to them both by having a different perspective, or more importantly, just listening to theirs. If our relationship was different and we were close, sister-like friends, I think I might have felt entirely shut out and excluded. The great, thrilling privilege of being their sister was that my place in their lives was established, and I had to respond to an exciting challenge. It was up to me to maintain the integrity of our relationship, while watching it take on a new shape.

Beth and Grace are, I think, closer than they have ever been because they have shared something profound. Yet I can share their experience in different ways. It's an honour to be a spare pair of hands, and sometimes be the one who dashes around the house looking for muslin squares, or an auxiliary cuddler and dinner supervisor, while a mum takes a phone call or goes to the loo. It's a duty and a joy, and it's made me realise that friendship can be about meeting someone's practical needs as well as their emotional ones. I'm a better, more helpful friend to both of them because I haven't been through the experience that they've shared. And while I still have pangs where I feel that I've 'lost' Grace to Beth, I have to remember that watching Beth experience parenthood has brought me closer to her.

Beth and I grew up constantly thinking of new ways to torture and antagonise each other. While we had moments of great tenderness and fun, they would rarely last beyond the five-minute mark, before someone tried to hit someone over the head with a section of wooden train track. But the birth of Penny has finally created common ground. We're both besotted with her baby, and our friendship has finally bloomed.

I'm also now a member of a secondary squad – the aunties. I'm forging a new friendship with Livvy, Maddy and Dotty because we're *not* mums, and I'm forced to rethink my big sister status anxiety because I don't really feel like the big sister any more. We have two big things in common – firstly, our love for our niece and nephew, and secondly, the fact that we can all go to the pub together without worrying about who is taking care of our niece and nephew. The babies are obviously great focus pullers. I could walk into the room with a Nobel Prize around my neck, as if it were Flavor Flav's clock necklace, and I'd still be upstaged by Arthur pooing on the carpet. This is absolutely as it should be – and Arthur's poo face is very sweet. But when I'm with my auntie squad, we all remind each other that our triumphs and disasters are still interesting and significant. We're not mothers yet, and we might not ever be, but as women, we don't need to be defined by the children in our lives, or by the lack of them.

When I was little, I found it really difficult to be friends with my sisters because of our differences, but as an adult, it's these differences that captivate me. It's baffling and brilliant – as if six seeds were planted from the same packet, into the same soil, and grew into a bouquet of wildflowers. I learn so much from my sisters and their different interests and perspectives. They're clever and wise. They constantly remind me that there are infinite ways to be a woman, and no right one. It charms and shocks me in equal measure. As adults, we've found the space to pursue different dreams and identities. It doesn't feel as though we're competing in the way we did when we were children, and this has allowed our friendship to flourish.

For me, competitiveness can be one of the most painful elements of friendship, and I think this is closely connected to the way I feel about my sisters. I wish I'd known that it was OK to be jealous of my sisters sometimes, and I think our friendship would have been stronger for longer if I'd acknowledged these feelings. When Grace won a *Blue Peter* badge, and got to sing a song about Vikings on TV, I would have been a much better, more enthusiastic friend if I'd allowed myself to think, 'I wish it was me, I would have liked that opportunity,' instead of pretending to myself that she was a loser, saying that everyone in my class had laughed at her, and you could barely even see her because she was hidden by a Viking shield. When Beth won a poetry competition I was so torn up with envy that I refused to watch her collect her prize. The rest of the family went for a lovely walk by the river, watched Beth on the quay, cheered her and ate delicious Cornettos. I sat in my room, sulking, squeezing blackheads and marinating in my own toxic cloud of envy.

It never occurred to me that my sisters might be jealous of any of my achievements. Sure, I was good at school, but I just assumed that they heard that I'd got full marks on a test and thought, 'What a nerd!' Looking back, I really wish we'd talked about it. We would have understood each other so much better if we'd been honest with each other about the way we endured triumphs and disasters. Instead, I pretended it didn't matter, and they didn't matter either. I don't think I fooled anyone.

As women, it can be incredibly hard to celebrate each other, and we don't always acknowledge that it's hard to see every female triumph as a win for the team. We love our friends, but we compare ourselves with them constantly, and I think that it's really difficult to address the fact that sometimes we're all secretly ranking ourselves in a way that can become a real friendship obstacle. Women are unique. Sisters are unique. The struggle comes from reconciling that uniqueness with the pursuit of common ground and celebrating each other without comparing ourselves.

However, my sisters all excel in one area that infuriates me, inspires me, and makes me desperate to keep up. They're all *funnier* than me. They have funny bones. Before she started school, Dotty was improvising and improving upon various dull hymns, once singing, deadpan, at the end of Mass, 'Tell blind people that they can see / And watch them walk into a tree.' Her twin Maddy has been compared, more than once, to Tommy Cooper. Livvy is devastatingly quick and has the sort of wit that could send rockets into space, Grace is a brilliant actress who can impersonate anyone, and Beth is truly gifted at finding the funny in the weird. They are the funniest people I know, and this has set the tone for all of my future friendships. I have lived my life pursuing people who are almost as much fun. I will forgive *anything* from a person who can make me laugh.

Funniness always works best as a group enterprise, and my sisters' talents are inclusive. Perhaps it's because we have such an intimate relationship, and we understand each other's rhythms and idiosyncrasies in a way we'd barely know how to articulate, but when we're being funny, we're better together. We know how to collaborate. I think that's what true friendship is – feeling united, being part of a group that makes you all feel bigger and stronger than the sum of all your parts. When I'm with them, and they're making me laugh, I have no desire to be the funniest, and I don't care about being the most of anything else. I'm just delighted to be part of the gang.

This can make our other friendships quite complicated. There are some of my sisters' friends that I adore, and some that would make me climb out of a top-floor window and throw myself to a grizzly, gravelly death, just to avoid having to be in the same room as them for an evening. There are some who have been so kind and gentle with my sisters that I feel as though I will be forever in their debt. It's as if I had been granted a tricky favour by the Mafia. One day, one of these people will show up on my doorstep with a baseball bat, saying, 'You know how I took Livvy home after she wet herself in PE when she was six? Well, one good turn deserves another!' and I'll find myself emptying out my life savings for them, or driving a getaway car from Plymouth to Aberdeen. I will agree to this without a moment's hesitation.

Then, there are some who have been cruel, dismissive or hurtful towards my sisters, and in the unlikely event that I had the opportunity to wreak violent revenge, I would do the time. There is a girl whose Facebook friendship request I refused because about fifteen years ago, she made a big, flirty, visible play for a boy that Grace liked, even though Grace was supposed to be one of her closest friends. If Facebook was more like TripAdvisor, I would have given her a one-star rating and a damning review. 'She's BAD, possibly EVIL, because she made a poor romantic decision when she was a teenager!' When I mentioned this to Grace, she had no memory of the event or even the boy she'd been into. I bring this level of misguided loyalty into my friendships too. There's a clothes shop I won't go into because they still owe my pal £275 of back pay from the summer of 2008, even though my friend still buys things from them and *pays for them*, ignoring my suggestion that she help herself to some stock and stroll out.

This is the worst and most intense way that being a sister informs my friendships. When I am close to someone who is, in my mind, wronged, I approach the issue with a great strength of feeling and little common sense, perhaps because when you're someone's sister, every negative incident that befalls them seems personal. As a friend, I'm Scrappy Doo. I'd like to be better at remembering birthdays, phoning for chats, helping out in a crisis and generally being kind and thoughtful. However, when it comes to getting offended on someone's behalf and meting out vigilante justice, I can't be beaten – as long as the friend feels suitably avenged by me making a Miss Piggy noise whenever their enemy's name is mentioned.

Rationally, I know that my sisters aren't perfect friends, any more than I am. They are just as capable of hurting someone as being hurt, and the chemistry of their friendships is private and unknowable, at least to me. I find it difficult to understand or even admit to myself that my sisters have friends who know them in a way I never can. Yet, hypocritically I share much more of myself with my friends than I do with my sisters. I think this is partly because we're desperate to protect each other from worry, but also because we fear that we won't be understood. How can I give Dotty unbiased advice that's tailored to a 25-year-old woman, and not distorted through my lens of 'eldest' girl helping her 'baby' sister? How can I tell them when I'm worried about work, or arguing with my husband, or having an existential crisis when I'm supposed to be the most grown up and knowing? As a friend and sister, I still find it deeply difficult to tell people I need help or even ask questions. I grew up believing that I needed to have all of the answers, or at least look as though I know what I'm doing. Clearly, I don't. The more I learn, the less I know. But I've been lucky to find friends who have encouraged me to be vulnerable, and this has helped me to become closer with my sisters.

Compared with sisterhood (in the biological sense), there is so much freedom in friendship. Of course, you've got to treat your friends with great care. Boundaries are erected and respected, and you can't rub up against each other in the same way, figuratively or literally. I needed to make friends in order to learn how to play nicely.

For me, biological sisterhood feels much more primal than friendship. Like lion cubs, we bonded by touch. Sisterhood permitted us to be close to each other, and rough with each other, forging an intimacy that I couldn't presume with even my dearest friends now. Yet, when I was little I often felt lonely. If I complained about a lack of friends, my parents would say, 'Your sisters are your friends,' which was confusing and, for a long time, not true.

I started school, and it seemed cold and scary. Connecting with the other children was confusing, and if anyone expressed an interest in being my friend, I'd often let them project a personality onto me. For Laura, I was an amateur ballerina, until our reception teacher expressed serious concern for the wellbeing of my toes. For Hayley, I became a dog lover, even though I was so scared of dogs that I burst into tears on her doorstep when I heard her Labrador barking and had to be taken home before tea. I didn't really understand the dynamics of friendship until I was in my twenties, and I'm still learning.

At secondary school, when I was free-floating and friendless, we were always being forced into assemblies about friendship groups. We were given passive-aggressive lectures from long-suffering teachers about bullying, the dangers of excluding each other, and what we needed to do when a group dynamic turns toxic. These were always being given for the benefit of a specific group of girls – Alex C, Alex H-S, Bryony, Leonie and Alice. At thirty-three, there is still nothing I wouldn't give for the apparent confidence of Alex H-S at sixteen. These girls were made of chewing gum and Lancôme lip gloss, when the rest of us kept babyish Bonne Bell Lip Smackers in our blazer pockets. Even though the school demanded that we wear scratchy grey socks pulled above our knees, they rolled them down to expose their slender shins – always tanned, never streaky. I still remember eavesdropping on their conversations – I was in the same GCSE history class as Alex H-S and Leonie – and hoarding clues, hoping that I could become sophisticated and beautiful by simply copying everything they said. Leonie was planning to dump her boyfriend before starting university, 'because I feel as though I've done my partying; I want to concentrate on studying, for the sake of my future career'. If anyone else had said that, they'd be branded the biggest nerd in the world, but Leonie was so revered that her words ended at least ten nascent relationships.

Still, our Famous Five were always fighting with each other. To everyone else in the school, they were too aloof and beautiful to approach, or even look at directly, but whenever I observed them from afar, I realised that they were sisters under the skin. Once, after school, I watched Bryony screaming at Alex C over a borrowed Biro, and then I was aware of Bryony's pointy ballet flat sailing over my head. I heard a rumour that they had been on a group holiday to Marbella, where Alice's uncle had an apartment, and one of the girls had been so infuriated by Alice's bossiness that she dipped Alice's mascara brush in her own poo. Frequently, the girls would gang up on each other, making each other miserable for months at a time, and yet no outsider would ever be allowed to infiltrate the group. They had a truly toxic squad, which functioned at a furious pace, yet they loved each other fiercely. I envied them this for a long time. It took me years to realise I had my own squad at home, and the fact that we'd all inherited each other didn't make our connection any less special. In fact, it might have been more special, in that no one did anything especially mean or disgusting with their own poo after the age of ten.

I think the problem with the squad is very similar to the problem of Communism. It's a lovely warm theory. Socialism is, ideally, like being in a family with millions of other people. This is great if the family is the Waltons, and less good if the family is a real one. A female friendship group are supposed to behave like perfect sisters, loving each other, supporting each other and rallying around during times of crisis. However, within the squad, there will be serious status anxiety and hair pulling. People clash, people feel left out, and people form alliances against other members. When you're in a gang with five other people, you take every fall out five times more personally than usual.

However, as I've gone from being a very unhappy child to a very contented adult, I've understood that friendship isn't about identity, popularity or proving unswerving loyalty. Very simply, it starts with truly appreciating someone's company. When I was younger, I'd antagonise my sisters and focus on the way that we clashed. Because of this, I didn't know which parts of my personality could possibly be appealing to anyone who wasn't forced to be my friend because we lived in the same house. There is something shocking and freeing about realising that you're allowed to seek people out and choose to spend time with them because they're likeable and fun.

Sisterhood can be claustrophobic, but there's so much freedom in a truly joyous friendship. I started to see aspects of my sisters in my new friends, which made me feel closer to everyone.

Confidence and self-esteem grows when people take you at your own estimation, rather than configuring the person in front of them with the person who once peed in their shared bathwater. Essentially, through my grown-up friends, I've learned how to be myself, and how to feel comfortable instead of contriving ways of being cool. It's utterly glorious to have women in my life who didn't know me when I was ten, and who don't have vivid memories of my Andrew Lloyd Webber phase. Their friendship is the warm sunlight that has allowed me to grow sturdy, secure and confident enough to become a better, kinder sister. Broadly speaking, our friends are the people who have taken us at our own estimation, and our sisters are the ones who still take us at their own estimation, but hopefully love and like us anyway.

When my friends spend time with my sisters, they treat them like rock stars. Sometimes they even ask for photos. It's adorable, and slightly overwhelming, but it makes sense. If you love someone, you're always excited to discover clues about who they are, and why. Meeting my sisters' friends is a thrill for the same reason, because it gives me a glimpse of a side of my sisters I rarely get to see. Visiting Dotty, the youngest, in her adopted hometown, Brighton, is fun, magical and deeply disturbing. My beautiful baby sister has become a gorgeous young woman with a job, a flat, a boyfriend, a social life and as far as I can tell, no desire to suddenly, unselfconsciously burst into the *Mulan* soundtrack. I never quite know how to deal with it, so I usually force her to let me buy lunch and a present from Topshop. As well as feeling a bit bewildered by the gap between the kid I think I know, and the adult that she's become, it's a struggle to understand that Dotty is the product of friendships with people who are not me. Her passions and choices have been influenced by people I don't know – all of my sisters have worked out who they are and discovered their independent spirits by spending time with other women. Their friends have helped them grow up, and have turned them into women I want to cultivate an adult friendship with. I ought to be grateful. Wholly irrationally, I sometimes feel left out, even though I know that my friends have done the same for me.

Still, the complications of friendship are eternal, and most of us will have periods where we hate our friends, we overthink our friendships and we convince ourselves that we're doing everything wrong. If you listen very carefully, and you're very quiet, right now you can probably hear a long-suffering teacher giving an assembly about When Friendship Groups Go Wrong. Somewhere, a maid of honour is giving a wedding speech and making a joke about how she didn't speak to the bride for a month because she threw a shoe at her.

Keeping one friendship going can be horribly hard, and it becomes exponentially harder when that friendship is part of a whole. Groups become bigger and more complicated than the sum of their parts. My sisters have taught me that it's OK to have separate connections within the same squad. You can worry and obsess over who your other friends are friends with. You can become a slave to status anxiety, and worry that you'll never find the true friend who passes the impossible test and proves their eternal love. You can panic about not feeling 'very close' to anyone, and never finding the friend who will volunteer to braid your hair. Or you can love the one you're with. You can take your friendships moment by moment, and instead of counting them by lifetimes, measure them by afternoons. Or not measure them at all. It's OK if your squad feels loose, and insufficiently sisterly, or if your biological sisters will not be corralled into providing photogenic proof of their love on your Instagram account. If you can find a way of enjoying someone's company, you can be their friend. That's enough.

Grace

Grace is my most gentle sister, and the fiercest one too. She has great poise, power and presence. I've never known her to go out of her way to court attention, but she demands it. That might be down to the power of good teacher training, but even before she started explaining physics to teenagers for a living, she's always given the impression that she's ready to start kicking ass and taking names. But first, she'll ask you how you take your tea.

She inspires deep, uncomplicated love in everyone who knows her. I think she's most like our mum in her sense of quiet but total capability. She gets things done, seemingly without breaking a sweat. She is also extremely, classically beautiful. All of my sisters are gorgeous, of course – but it was Grace's face that caused me the most envy and distress during my teenage years. Her lips are a little fuller than mine, her cupid's bow more cartoonish. Where my nose gives up and lazily collapses in the middle of my face, hers bravely goes the extra elegant millimetre. When I read about girls in books with peachy complexions, hers is the skin I see. Her temper is rarely provoked, but when she's angry, she becomes steel and ice. The rage is entirely contained within her voice and never troubles her lovely forehead, which means she'll look twenty-five for the next twenty years, when I'm so quick to frown that the space around each eye is already starting to resemble a relief map of the Scottish Highlands.

For a long time, I believed Grace's beauty made her brave. She has always seemed invulnerable and inviolate, a swan on the water who always got what she wanted. This was partly because she used to exist, in my imagination, as the sort of noble fairy tale heroine who will always choose the humble straw casket over the bejewelled treasure chest, biblically meek where I was grubby and grabby. She deserved rubies and castles, even though she would have been content in a cottage with a woodcutter. Growing up, there were moments when I believed that I would be glad to see her fail. However, I've seen her heart break over and over again, and felt mine break with it.

When Grace started trying to get pregnant, we all lazily assumed that motherhood would be almost instant, and instantly fulfilling. Partly because Grace was, at twenty-seven, practically a child herself, and for her womb, growing a baby would come as easily as growing cress comes to a flannel. Partly because we were frightened lapsed Catholics who wouldn't look at a sperm cell through a microscope without wearing a full body condom, just in case we were punished, with pregnancy, for our sinful prurience. But mostly because this was *Grace*. Grace never ever asked the universe for anything she didn't feel that she deserved, and it was her innate goodness that won her all of those lead roles and debating trophies. Surely motherhood, the only job she ever truly wanted, was a state she wouldn't even have to fill in an application form for? Maybe she'd be headhunted, like the Virgin Mary!

Darling Gracie had just got past the three-month mark and euphorically shared her happy news when she lost her first baby. She'd been due to give birth on my wedding day. All six of us were filled with feeling that had no outlet or direction. We were all young, naïve and obnoxious enough to believe the world would work for us, that disappointment was temporary, that we could speak to the manager, or to *their* manager, and demand that any mistake could be rectified to everyone's satisfaction. After all, we were going to make excellent aunties! But we could only sob for what we felt we had lost, but most of all, for Grace. Sometimes it simply isn't useful or helpful to point out bright sides or silver linings, and it's not kind to minimise loss by telling someone you love to look at their gains. All you can do is say that the universe is a bastard, and that you'd like to raze it to the ground and build a new one on their behalf. That you truly believed your love could protect them from pain, but it couldn't, and you're so, so sorry.

Like a good fairy tale heroine, Grace blinked back tears

and kept trying, and trying. (Please stop thinking about my little sister having sex, or I'll have to murder you.) And baby Arthur, a cousin for Penelope, a singer of songs, a teller of stories, and an eater of other people's cardigans, was born almost exactly two years later.

In motherhood, Grace has become more like herself than I have ever known her. She is even more gentle, and even more fierce. Her jaw is soft, her skin more peach-like, her observations smarter and her jokes even sillier. She has produced a tiny person who makes me love him so ferociously that I can't look at him without worrying about going into cardiac arrest, and I'm only an auntie. Grace deserves everything she wants, but I think she feels as though she's already got the bejewelled treasure chest. Arthur is, at the time of writing, not yet able to speak in sentences, but he's already the recipient of one of life's greatest prizes. He has Grace for a mum.

Grace facts

○ Grace can do an eerily perfect impression of Dr Zoidberg, the lobster from *Futurama*.

○ She is, I think, the only one of my sisters who ever impulsively rings up for a chat.

○ Possibly out of necessity, Grace is the best chef and baker, and once taught us all to make Christmas cake pops. Grace's were the only ones that actually looked like reindeers, although mine confusingly tasted like venison.

○ As a student, Grace was an enthusiastic member of the university Gilbert and Sullivan society and if you give her a third gin and tonic, she'll sing, 'I am the very model of a modern major general.'

- We organised each other's hen parties, ostensibly because we lived the nearest to each other and it seemed practical, but really, because we were the only sisters who could trust each other to make sure that everyone had fun and no one was frightened by a surprise stripper.

- Not only did Grace agree to have her picture taken with me for a *Grazia* feature, she took her knickers off when the photographer said they were spoiling the line of her dress.

- Grace loves audiobooks of very old-fashioned murder mysteries, especially mad posh ones when everyone sounds like Celia Johnson and says, 'Halp! Halp! Something rilly offul hes heppened!'

CHAPTER TEN
Womanhood and Girl-on-Girl Judgement

I'd like to be able to tell you that having little sisters has made me an open-minded, all-embracing, judgement-free zone. I can't. However, I've spent some time trying to make sure that I quash or question the judgement before it forms on my tongue. Why do women judge other women, when we're all ultimately just trying to get along and survive in a universe in which we all seem to spend most of our time struggling to get tights on over freshly moisturised legs?

I judge my sisters because I love them, and I struggle with the idea that we're not all one person. I don't want them to get hurt, I don't want anyone to think badly of them and I don't want anyone to think badly of me, because they have assumed that we all behave in the same way. It's completely irrational, yet I don't think the issue is restricted to biological sisters. I judge Theresa May all the time, because even though we have next to nothing in common, I don't want people to think that other women are Brexit-enabling, anti-immigration-minded, wheatfield-loving people wearing whimsical shoes. It's OK for me to disagree with every single one of her policies; it isn't OK for me to write her off because of her predilection for kitten heels.

If you're a woman in the public eye, millions of other women are probably judging you. I often write about reality TV, and I'm stunned by the usually smart, compassionate women who tell me that they can't stand it because they hate seeing other women with fake tans and false eyelashes. When I start to unpick it, I realise it isn't about straightforward bitchiness, but chronic insecurity. As women, we're made to feel as though we're under constant and terrifying levels of scrutiny. It isn't just that we have high standards to meet – we have *a* high standard to meet. We need to be slim, clear-skinned, thick-lashed and pouty, intriguingly sexy without suggesting we would ever, ever show our nipples in an emergency or during a dare. We need to be knowledgeable about current affairs without going on about it, smart enough to run a business but not so smart as to frighten the horses, or potential husbands, and able to drink a single glass of red wine without demanding a second, or allowing our tongues to turn into a black Fruit Pastille. We need to have children, but not too many. We must have sex, but we can't really talk about it. And we're not meant to have visible sauce stains on our jumpers.

Even if, on a surface level, you're able to say, 'This is bullshit! Watch me pour ketchup straight into my mouth, patriarchy!', the pernicious, unspoken, relentless demands will have some impact on all of us, in some way. We're made to feel as though the world will end if we don't follow the rules – or rather, the world will cast us out and exclude us, and we'll spend an eternity spinning through fuzzy black infinity if anyone ever finds out exactly how much time we spend plucking our chins. We're like ballet dancers, landing on pointes soundlessly, breaking our bones and expected to tolerate this pain, to dance ourselves clean, over and over again until we're perfect. And when we see women who either seem to find it easier than we do to be perfect, or women who are visibly disobeying the rules that we've been destroying ourselves to follow, we judge them. When women seem to be colluding to make an already unreachably high standard even less possible for everyone else, we judge them. This is why I was guilty of thinking of some seriously unsisterly, unfeminist thoughts when the model Emily Ratajkowski was photographed bathing naked in a vat of spaghetti, an act that was framed by the media as one of female empowerment.

Ratajkowski is a year younger than my sister Liv. If Liv was an internationally successful model and starred in a series of sexy spaghetti photos, would I feel differently about the issue? Firstly, I have to admit that I'm jealous. If I had a body that was, in the eyes of twenty-first-century society, a tenth as sexy and desirable as Ratajkowski's is, I would be on all fours and daubing myself with Dolmio before you could say, 'That's a spicy meatball!' I'm insecure, I'm a narcissist, and I find it impossible to admire Ratajkowski's body without wondering what's 'wrong' with mine. If she were my little sister, the envy would probably feel much, much worse. The image of unreachable perfection would feel much closer to home, and I'd be quicker to take a personal negative from someone else's positive.

The other response I have, which I feel so keenly that it makes me wonder whether Ratajkowski really is my long-lost sister, is to lie face down on the floor and kick my legs and scream, 'IT'S NOT FAIR!' It's not fair that she falls so perfectly into this narrow, arbitrary definition of what is beautiful and sexy when so many of us feel that we're not even in the same postcode. It's not fair than she's contributing to that definition and, arguably, making things so much harder for women who already feel as though they have it tough. It's not fair that millions of people believe that her beauty is a greater, more significant asset than being clever, or funny, or kind. But is it fair to expect her not to use a great gift? If we all went to bed tonight and woke up tomorrow looking like *Sports Illustrated* models, would we all think, 'It is important that I don't become part of the problem, and I need to make sure that I don't become a stick with which other women are beaten?' Before we judge other women, we must walk a mile in their dinner.

I think we're especially judgemental when it comes to bodies and sexiness, and some of that judgement has a protective quality. When I was a teenager, my mum was constantly criticising my clothes, a judgement she'd soften with the words: 'I don't want anyone to get the wrong idea about you.' This is a universal conversation that predates the invention of Topshop, and mothers and daughters have been enduring it for decades. Yet I vividly remember how it made me feel – accused, persecuted, hot with shame. Mum was simply trying to protect me from the judgement of others, and I think this is at the root of the way we judge each other. Yet at the time, that judgement made me feel as though every single one of my desires and choices were wrong, but not so wrong that she was right. I wanted to be sexy, I wanted to be seen, and I wanted to believe that I could make the whole horrible ordeal go away if I simply covered up my clothes with giant, baggy sweatshirts. I thought she was being mean, and telling me my body was wrong. It didn't occur to me that the idea of being judged was why my exposed skin felt so itchy.

For a long time, I learned nothing. I couched my judgement as 'sisterly advice', which became a code for: 'I'm going to say something really horrible, that will make you feel terrible, but you can't cry about it because I care about your *self-improvement*!' Recently on WhatsApp, Grace revealed that she still remembers crying when she was too young to wear a bra, and Beth and I told her to change her top because you could see her nipples through it. Once, I made an unsolicited offer to Beth, suggesting I could nip to the chemist for her and buy some Jolen bleach. 'I don't know if you realised, but you're getting a bit of a moustache.'

Most of us spend more time looking at our own faces than anyone else does. Unless you're in a music video with Lionel Ritchie, and sculpting his head, there probably isn't anything that anyone can tell you about the way you look that will be news to you. It's simply mean and sneaky to make an unsolicited comment about someone else's appearance. When it comes to our own sisters, we think we can overstep the mark, but just because someone is of our blood, we can't tell them that they've gained weight or that their roots need doing. We're not giving them good news. We're saying, 'You have failed, and I value myself more highly than you for not failing in this way.'

How can we stop judging our biological and spiritual sisters? We need to give ourselves, and each other, a big break. Instead of having impossibly high standards for ourselves and inflicting those standards on other people, it's time to lower the bar. We've convinced ourselves that judgement is an act of love, and that it's a way of protecting and helping people who don't know any better. Maybe they just know differently. My sisters and I are six similar women who are actually very, very different from each other. We've had almost identical early experiences and opportunities, and yet not one of us has chosen the same path as the other. Beth and Grace both made the choice to be mothers, but they have very different parenting styles. I've never seen them judging each other for doing anything differently from each other, not even in a way that makes the judgement look like advice. But I've noticed that they both judge themselves in a way that's based on the imaginary judgement of the other one.

In her brilliant book *Yes Please*, Amy Poehler wrote that if women have one motto or refrain that they should etch on their brains, it should be: 'Good for her, not for me.' It means, good for Emily Ratajkowski, in her spaghetti! Her work has nothing to do with yours, and it doesn't mean that you need to get your bum out and be told that you're not enough. (In my case, my bum really is more than enough.) It means that one mum might choose to feed her children Turkey Twizzlers, and another mum might feed her child organic barley stew, and neither decision has anything to do with you unless the child throws food at you, in which case you can thank Turkey Twizzler mum for choosing the food that's much easier to get out of your hair. It means that you have no grounds to think badly of a woman who chooses to marry Piers Morgan or a semi-professional cage fighter, because you cannot know anything about the circumstances that leads a woman to make those decisions unless *you are her*. It means that we need to come together in seeing the separateness of our sisters, and understand that womanhood is infinitely wide. Other women don't exist to validate our decisions, and we have no business shaming and judging the ones whose paths run in an opposite direction to ours.

There is a myth that our sisters know us as well as we know ourselves, perhaps better. This myth stops us from succeeding, because it makes us wait to act, and leaves us wondering how we might be judged for it. Every time we judge a woman for doing something we wouldn't have done, we're judging ourselves harshly too. In order to let go of that, we must accept that every sister and woman in our lives has an unknowable quality. When women we'll never meet are constantly being judged on TV, online, in newspapers and magazines, it's easy to start believing in the lie that judgement is our job, that millions of women are too dumb to be fully informed about their own lives, and that we know best. We must challenge this idea every time we notice it. Let she who has never noticed a missed strip of hair on a newly shaved shin cast the first stone. Also, it doesn't matter if you've been a woman's roommate and wombmate, if you've cried in each other's arms during your first viewing of *E.T.*, if you've helped each other write inky letters to Father Christmas, if you've bitten down hard on each other's tender flesh, and made up within the hour. You can never, ever, *ever* tell her to bleach her moustache.

CHAPTER ELEVEN

Millennial Women and the Anxiety Epidemic

I t took me a long, long time to realise that I wasn't normal. That not everyone lies awake at night thinking about the end of the world, and they definitely weren't looking forward to the end of the world and freedom from endless, obsessive worrying. That they didn't creep downstairs, after everyone had gone to bed, to check that the oven wasn't still on, about to burn the house down, and then lie in bed and think about whether they should go back and check again, just in case they accidentally turned it on during the checking. They didn't cry over spilled milk, and they definitely didn't cry because their mothers had sprayed Dettol on the carpet to prevent a stain from setting, and they feared they might have accidentally ingested some of the Dettol and poisoned themselves. They did not worry when they went to school because they weren't there to stop their baby sisters from crawling under the sink and burying their heads into a lifetime's supply of plastic carrier bags.

As well as growing up believing that I was responsible for everyone's feelings, I believed that it was up to me to maintain basic levels of safety. As a reader, a worrier, and the child of two people who loved telling stories, but sometimes feared fear itself, I was blessed and cursed with a chronically overactive imagination. Saturday mornings at the swimming pool were deeply stressful because I decided it was my job to stop everyone from drowning. I was *delighted* when other children pooed in the pool and forced everyone out of the water because it meant leaving early, and knowing I'd only need to patrol a body of water if someone had a bath. One family holiday, we stayed in a windmill in Norfolk where the stairs were steep, and the sitting room was on the first floor. Maddy and Dotty were not quite walking, and so I held myself like a Navy SEAL, constantly tensed to stop, drop and create a full body barricade if either of them looked at the stone staircase, because I was so scared that they were going to fall.

I still can't strike a match, because of a deeply harrowing video I watched about fire safety when I was eight, featuring a careless cartoon bumblebee. I didn't really enjoy sex until I was twenty-two, because it took me six years of doing it before I could be absolutely sure that I wouldn't become instantly pregnant, then get sent back in time to 1732 to a home for unwed mothers, before being drowned in a well. I am obsessively, fundamentally frightened that some unknown horror will befall me, and the only way I can prevent this is by constantly playing a deeply damaging version of 'What if?', obsessively checking my email outbox in case I called anyone a cunt in my sleep, being late because I keep setting off and then running home to make sure I locked the door, and hoarding old train tickets as alibis, just in case someone with my name and face gets accused of murder and I need to be able to say where I was at 2.45 p.m. on 9 June 2015.

Essentially, my life constantly feels like being in that dream where you have to do A-level Latin, naked.

On a good day, I can deal with it. Over the last few years, I have worked very, very hard to challenge the panicky, self-loathing voice that believes everything I touch will turn out to be poisonous and flammable. But for a long time, I thought this was what it was to be 'good'. When my teachers praised me for being 'conscientious', I thought they were saying, 'She is careful. Nothing will be razed to the ground on her watch.' I took on too much responsibility with too much enthusiasm. But then, so did my sisters. They internalised my anxieties, and added their own. To this day, Beth is a Web MD self-administered torture junkie, Grace believes that she is responsible for everyone's good time, Livvy gets squirrelly and secretively anxious, claiming 'Everything's fine!' in a Freddie Mercury falsetto, Maddy spins out and struggles when she is confronted with any evidence that she is a human, not a machine, and Dotty would sometimes rather do nothing than risk getting it wrong. We're not all like this, all of the time, but our anxieties are like the herpes virus. The moment we're feeling vulnerable or run down, they play up, and when the telltale tingle begins, it's too late to stop it, we just have to ride it out.

My sisters and I are part of the most anxious generation on record. I've sat on panels where the source of this anxiety has been debated and minimised. Some people think that when we're struggling to find jobs, dealing with a housing crisis and under pressure to document every moment of the day in an envy-inducing way, that we deserve every atom and ounce of sympathy thrown at us, and that it's admirable that we haven't gone out onto the street with flaming torches and pushed for a full-scale social revolution. (I reckon everyone else saw that video, and my entire generation is just too frightened of fire.) Others think we're whiny little shits and we should think on, and if we went down a mine we'd have something to cry about. These people have inevitably retired from managing a hedge fund and live in a luxury duplex in Marbella where they complain if they have to read a menu in Spanish.

Do we genuinely have more to worry about, or have we simply evolved to a point of self-involvement at which we're acutely attuned to every heart-racing blip? Has every other generation been every bit as anxious, but not known that their feelings have a name, and just screamed into a cushion every time the build up became impossible to bear?

I think that there are plenty of ways in which life is challenging for my sisters and me, in a way it wasn't for our parents. To me, it seems as though there is an enormous amount of pressure on all of us, and fewer opportunities to do well. In some ways it's been much harder for us to find homes and jobs, and these are supposed to be the guide ropes that show us where to set up the rest of our lives, and how to do it.

Still, I know that while I've been deeply anxious about my work and living arrangements, they have been prompts for my worries, rather than the root of them. Grace has a life that I've coveted to the point of pain, during my most insecure moments. But having a job, a loving partner and a place on the property ladder – the triumvirate of goals for so many millennials, the hat trick of impossible dreams – doesn't make her immune to anxiety, and I suspect there are times when she feels she has more to worry about than the rest of us. Beth doesn't really bother with a social media presence, and this is supposed to be a recipe for contentment, but I know she feels panic in her bones. In different ways, I think Livvy, Maddy and Dotty are anxious about the future. What if nothing stays the same – and what if *everything* does?

Broadly speaking, the greatest challenge to our collective mental health is that we all have to be human beings. The causes of our anxiety aren't new, but we're responding to them more keenly than previous generations, or rather, we're not responding at all. We're sobbing, shaking and hiding under tables, muttering that we actually can't even. Where our parents see a frustrating email from a grumpy boss, or a phone bill that should have been paid two days ago, we see a fanged, furious monster.

I've learned that my anxiety is caused by very low self-esteem. Writing that makes me feel like the queen of the eighties. I really should be wearing a pastel shell suit, sitting on a pastel sofa, telling Maury Povich all about it while I cry into my frosted perm. But it's a real eighties problem. Broadly speaking, me and my sisters were part of the first generation who were bred to worry in a fairly focused way. Our older cousins, aunties, uncles and grandparents would be sent out to play in the road every night, with instructions to try not to get hit by a car before teatime. We were taught to stay indoors because everything in the road was dangerous. We'd be *lucky* to get run over; it was more likely that we'd end up getting besieged by paedophiles. It was much better if we came inside and did our homework, because we needed to work very, very hard if we wanted to go to university in ten years. If we didn't go to university, we'd never get good jobs, and then we'd remain in a state of arrested development, still at home, forever fearing the mythical road paedos.

Many of us have the false impression that someone with high self-esteem, or even healthy self-esteem, is a bit of a twat. For a long time I didn't understand what self-esteem is – having a sense of general happiness and a broadly positive sense of self that isn't dependent on other people's love or admiration. I thought it was shorthand for being a bit up yourself and getting too proud and complacent about your achievements. So much of my anxiety was and is centred around the idea that I might start getting something very wrong after getting it right. That I'm only worth talking to because of what I've acquired. Sometimes this has been grades, sometimes work, sometimes my body and sometimes my relationships. My sisters and I have all faced the same struggle at times. We're overachievers with eating and body issues, women who often wonder whether we fall short of the world's definition of likeable and lovable. Our parents and teachers put a *lot* of pressure on us, with the best of intentions. We were told we had potential to fulfil, which is a wonderful thing to hear. Yet, I think we were all made to feel as though it wasn't enough to be who we were. We had to show them what we were going to do with that potential, in order to be worth anything.

Then, these messages were compounded by myriad sources – the world is full of people who go out of their way to shatter women's self-esteem. We're told, over and over again, that we've no business valuing ourselves by just *being*.

We are what we eat, who we date, where we work, the number of people who follow us on social media. And when we succeed within the narrowest of parameters, when we've measured ourselves against a million different metrics and come out on top, it doesn't count for anything unless we keep doing it over, and over, and over again.

Getting permission to like yourself, as a woman, is exhausting. This is why Grace sometimes defines herself as a 'crap mum', why Maddy struggled with being single when the rest of us were in relationships, and why I sometimes cry myself to sleep if I haven't met my self-imposed target of workouts and word counts. We women in our twenties and thirties have grown up in a world where we're encouraged to be exceptional – but we can't just *be*. When our sense of who you are is contingent on checking an increasing number of boxes, you're only ever one missed barre class away from a breakdown. I don't think I know any women who haven't experienced some form of debilitating anxiety, or other mental health issues. I'm sure it's because our lives have become impossible to survive because we're always being told that we're not good enough to live them.

Sometimes, I bring my low self-esteem and anxiety to my role as sister. I feel guilty about not being proactive enough, not planning enough meetings and events for us, not phoning to check in and not giving my sisters enough gifts. I approach it as though I might be ranked, and if I'm really, really good I might win some John Lewis vouchers for being Sister of the Month. However, being a sister is a great cure for shonky self-esteem. There are no prizes. All you have to do is show up. You can't be bad at being a sister. You can be flaky, or mean, or boring, but you're *still* a sister, and you're no less of a sister than you are when you're prompt and organised about birthday cards.

It is lovely to have a part of my identity that isn't contingent on how I feel or how I behave. I know my sisters feel the same, partly because when we're together, we all know exactly who we are, and partly because we don't place any conditions or expectations on each other. I'm not capable of judging Beth and Grace's parenting styles; I couldn't even if I wanted to. I'd only think about intervening if they left the babies in Wetherspoons with a pitcher of Blue Lagoon and change for the cigarette machine.

Sometimes, I wonder whether anyone else feels as though they have been sent out on a long and impossible quest by a very grumpy wizard who hasn't actually told them what they're looking for, and just checks in every so often to say, 'No, not that. You're doing it wrong.' But I know that my anxiety is especially bad when I put myself under a lot of pressure to achieve, and that the anxiety is much more manageable when I remember that I don't need to *do* anything in order to be a perfectly acceptable human adult.

I would do anything to grant my sisters the permanent power of self-esteem – not the sense that they're exceptional and amazing, and other people are lucky to know them, even though I do believe that. But something sturdier and more solid. The idea that they do not need to overachieve in order to be liked and loved. That they can use their considerable talents to gratify their own sense of curiosity and ambition, instead of spunking their energy on the most impossible task, trying to earn the world's conditional love and approval.

Millennial Women and the Anxiety Epidemic

It makes sense that women are prone to bouts of anxiety, because we're constantly receiving unsolicited feedback on what we're doing and how well we're doing it. Perhaps the best way to boost self-esteem is to work out a way of tuning out that feedback, while questioning the agendas of the people who offer it and making sure that we're never the ones who are supplying it. Anxiety is insidious, and I've noticed that all of my sisters become anxious and unsure about everything they do when they've been on the receiving end of some unsolicited criticism. Once, when Beth was ten and very self-conscious, our parish priest asked her to give a reading during Mass. Beth took some persuasion, partly because she didn't want to do it unless she believed she could do it perfectly. If she'd had more self-esteem, she would have leaped up, had a go and laughed off the fact that it's quite hard to pronounce 'Gethsemane' when you've only ever seen it written down.

She was nervous, but she was great – until a very grumpy man cornered her afterwards and shouted at her for speaking too fast. Poor Beth. Watching her reaction was like seeing David Attenborough make a time-lapse documentary about puberty. Her shoulders slumped, her gaze went straight to the floor and she avoided speaking in public until we were well into the millennium. Part of the problem was that Beth had been brought up to please grown-ups, and told that their opinion mattered, and was instrumental in defining how she could feel about herself. The other part of the problem was that this particular grown-up must have known it. Most of our anxieties can be traced back to parents, school and cultural concerns. For my sisters and me, I think a good 40 per cent is connected to things that bossy old men said to us at church. What would Jesus do?!

As women, and sisters in spirit, I think that we need to be more honest and open about the fact that so many of us have a problem with self-esteem. It's time to question the causes, and the messages we hear that make us feel as though we're only worth liking and loving if our success can be measured in a certain way. We need to find ways to acknowledge and appreciate each other that aren't contingent on achievement. This is partly because I think that our achievements will become so much bigger and more interesting if we're not using them to try to please people. When we like ourselves in a happy, healthy, relaxed way, and when we stop being anxious about *not* achieving, and worrying about the world ending, we can fly.

Liv

Liv is my negative. She's dark where I'm blonde, pale where I'm tanned, narrow where I'm wide and bone where I'm flesh. Yet, we look more like each other than any other sister pairing. We both have a nose that dips down slightly, and a left eye that opens a little more widely than the right. When we laugh, the laugh starts at the centre of our faces, and erupts outwards. When we're angry, our features turn to stone, but our pupils constrict to pinpricks. And we cry loudly and lavishly, with very little prompting, although Liv is much more self-conscious about it than I am.

When Liv was born in 1990, she was really, really ill. At the time, my sisters and I were too little to fully understand what was going on (she had a diaphragmatic hernia). Tissue was growing inside Liv's lungs, and she struggled to breathe properly. She was home for a bit, then whisked off to the John Radcliffe hospital. For a while, Beth genuinely believed that the JR had been chosen because their canteen sold a particularly excellent jam doughnut.

Sometimes I wonder whether Liv feels like the middliest of middle children because after her birth we all felt sad and strange. The first few months of her life were miserable and worrying for everyone. We'd just moved to Buckinghamshire because Dad had been transferred to the London office. He was commuting, leaving in darkness, coming back just before bedtime while worrying about the effects of the recession, and how to support his growing family. Now I know that there was a bullying environment at work and Dad was often tasked with firing large groups of people, while constantly being made to worry about whether he was going to be fired himself. Mum was also suddenly stuck in a remote and fairly snobby village in the heart of the commuter belt. There wasn't a single local shop in walking distance. I was having a horrible time at my new school, and Beth and Grace were just old enough to feel freaked out and confused by the disruption to their routine.

I was just five years old, and I felt completely alone. Every morning I woke up feeling fearful, wondering what the bullies would do to me and knowing that the problems would start as soon as I stepped on the school bus, with no one letting me sit next to them, and the driver shouting at me for not sitting down. Still, I sensed that as a family, we had bigger, sadder problems, gathering like dark clouds. I didn't want to make things worse, so I kept quiet. I remember that awful period as a time of hushed voices and overheard conversations that made no sense to me. It's only now that I realise that we struggled to bond because it felt as though she came into my life at the point that everything in it seemed to start going wrong. At the time, I felt like the bad big sister in a fairy story, cast into the wilderness because of the arrival of a more vulnerable, more beloved new sibling. As I've grown up, I've realised that neither of us were to blame – but I'm incredibly proud of the relationship we've forged in spite of it all, and that as adults, we've worked out a way to love each other.

It took us a long time to be close, and I still feel as though she's the sister I understand the least. Liv was the most rebellious teenager, and at the time Beth and I were infuriated by the way she seemed to revel in drama. We had our moments of wildness, but we were always careful about being caught. Liv was a conspicuous smoker and was caught having cigarettes at the bottom of the garden, and once upstairs in her bedroom. She'd throw her school bag on the sofa and a packet of Malboro Gold would tumble out. Somewhere, there are toddlers stealing chocolate buttons who are sneakier and more subtle than Liv. It took me a long time to realise that she wanted to be seen, and none of us were very good at seeing her. That being the little sister of Beth, Grace and me was *really hard*, and trying to be the 'bad' sister was much more fun than following in our footsteps.

However, Liv really isn't the bad sister. She's deeply kind

and instinctively generous. She's very intuitive – she can read a room, and she gravitates towards the quieter people, who need love, attention and company without knowing how to ask for it. She's naturally intelligent, and has a real gift for making quick connections, retaining information and evaluating it. She's also one of the hardest workers I know. Some people believe that everyone should be a waiter, bar tender or shop assistant for at least a year, as a form of National Service – because it helps you to understand people better and will make sure that you always tip properly. Liv was one of the most motivated and long-serving part-time waitresses I've ever known (perhaps partly because pocket money doesn't pay for many cigarettes) but it left her with a legacy of great grace. Liv listens, she makes people feel cared for, and she rarely complains without due cause.

One of the greatest privileges of watching Liv become a young woman has been seeing her find her style. In different ways, we've all used clothes to try to work out how we're different from each other, and sometimes been stymied and stifled by sharing and hand-me-downs. Now, I realise that Liv's clothes give me clues to her personality that I should have picked up on a while ago. She's feminine, arty, creative and still a little bit rebellious – and you will know her by her cascading, Calder-esque earrings, her borrowed band tees and exposed hipbones, her pretty, preppy winter coat and her fondness for found sunglasses.

Like me, Liv (and her lovely boyfriend Ed) live by the coast, and from her sitting room you can see the sea. Like me, Liv can behave quite bravely when she doesn't completely feel it, she can force herself to get up at six in the morning to do something she doesn't want to do, and she'll always feel better for it. She loves a dare, she reads when she's lonely and she's utterly, unshakeably loyal. I wish I'd appreciated our similarities sooner and been a kinder and more compassionate sister. She's very precious. There was a point when we didn't know whether or not we'd have her in our lives for this long. Every day spent with Liv is a lucky one.

Liv facts

○ Liv's legacy from her life-threatening childhood illness is an ability to deliver truly toxic, noxious farts. She's a one-woman chemical warfare unit. She could replace Trident. She is deeply proud of this.

○ In Swanage, Liv's role in *The Frog Prince* is still talked about. She played Grace's body double in the last scene, in order to give the impression that Grace transformed from frog to prince in half a second, cloaked by the emissions from a hired smoke machine. Few people know the secret.

○ She has invested more time, effort and energy in learning all of the words to all of the songs in *Hamilton* than most people apply to their full-time jobs.

○ For her fourteenth birthday, she got her first mobile phone. It lasted for about five hours before she destroyed it at Thorpe Park, by taking it on the log flume.

○ Her favourite Disney film is *The Great Mouse Detective*. She's especially fond of a sexy mouse character who sings a totally inappropriate song which features the refrain, 'Hey fellas, tonight's the night!' As a child she used to sing it in the bath until her watery high kicks started a leak in the kitchen ceiling.

○ Liv has never forgotten anyone else's birthday – she remembers dates as other people remember their ten times table.

CHAPTER TWELVE

Family Car Journeys, a Love Letter

To understand the genesis of my love/hate relationship with my little sisters, you need to know about the car journeys.

For children, travelling *en famille* is essentially training for being in a hardcore band. Someone is constantly crying while everyone else takes turns to be sick. We have spent hours congealing together, a collective, sweaty blur of punching, screaming and crumbs. Occasionally the acrid cheesy cloud of vomit would disperse as Dad opened the window and created his own acrid smoky cloud of Rothmans. Just as we thought our stomachs had settled, there would be a petrol stop, prompting us all to roll our eyes like dying swans, before making a great, theatrical show of breathing into pillows and duvets. Sometimes Beth would say, 'We've been doing a book about chemical warfare at school. You could probably drown someone in petrol. Imagine this being the last thing you ever smelled!' and the tears would course down our faces. Sometimes the vomit would course down our chins too.

However, I adored family car journeys, because all I ever wanted was to live in a Broadway musical, and that's how I experienced the back seat. Endless, contrived and implausible

drama, punctuated by near-constant song. I sang my heart out
from Shropshire to Chester, then Bournemouth to
Buckingham and back. I could sing for thousands of miles. I'd
perfected a seven song set that I was happy to share with
every single patron of the Little Chef at the Oxford Services.

Singing separated my sisters and brought us together. I'd
bellow along to ABBA, closing my eyes and believing that my
rendition of 'Slipping Through My Fingers' was unique, my
interpretation of the verse saturated in pathos – then Beth
and I would bellow the chorus together, our eyes locked on
each other with love, even though just five minutes ago we'd
been trying to slip each other's fingers through the tops of the
electric windows before pushing the button.

The car was where our sentimental education took place.
I learned about heartbreak from pop songs that were written
before I was born, becoming familiar with the intimate
feelings of people I'd never meet. Away from the car, we were
all forbidden from learning anything about adult experiences
or emotions. *Neighbours* and *Grange Hill* were considered to
be too racy to be suitable for our childish eyes. Mum and
Dad would wrap their forearms around our faces in
newsagents, lest we catch a glimpse of sexy Sallie-Anne
sharing her vital statistics with the *Daily Star.* Anything
connected with sex and relationships was spelled out, not said.
Sometimes we'd overhear that old family friends were getting
D-I-V-O-R-C-E-D, like Tammy Wynette. Yet the moral code
was different in the car. You could do anything with anyone,
as long as it was set to music. When we were all on wheels,
our parents' taste was only catholic with a lower case 'c'.

We all had favourites, or rather, songs that resonated

especially with us. Beth did a beautiful, eerily knowing version of Petula Clark's 'Don't Sleep in the Subway', relishing the dropped 'g' of 'darlin''. Grace loved Annie Lennox. We became obsessed with the Beach Boys, not because we were cool enough to appreciate *Pet Sounds*, but because one of us had acquired an album of Beach Boys songs, sung entirely by the Muppets. There are thousands of reasons to love and adore the Beach Boys, but my first was that their songs can be divided democratically. Everyone had space to shine separately, and everyone could come together for the chorus. I've heard that the band's relationships were sometimes only harmonious in a musical sense – but they brought love and peace to my sisters and me, occasionally for almost five minutes at a time. Then, there was ABBA.

This was long before the *Mamma Mia!* era, and the peak of the ABBA revival. I gather that you weren't even allowed to like ABBA ironically in the early nineties. My parents had loved them and listened to them when they were growing up, and so the tapes made their way into the car and into my ears. I didn't know what ABBA looked like, and I didn't always know what they were singing about, but I fell in love with them immediately. I loved them in a way that I didn't fully understand. It was an entirely one-sided relationship, but Agnetha, Anni-Frid, Björn and Benny were the first people I truly connected with emotionally beyond my family.

When my sisters were hitting me, or each other, I'd float away from the group and imagine my life as the fifth member of the band – and whether they would prefer to change their name to ABBAD, or DABBA. Even though I was in the middle of my own little gang of siblings, I longed to be in theirs, wearing thoughtfully coordinated sequins that weren't covered in crumbs, or someone else's sick. The lyrics to 'Super Trouper' mesmerised me, and made me yearn for something I couldn't quite articulate. Imagine being exhausted from being the centre of attention, instead of being exhausted by the act of constantly trying to attract attention. Imagine having someone special, to pick out from a crowd, and not feeling as though you were always a vague and indistinguishable part of a sea of faces.

Twenty-five years after I fell in love with ABBA, in the back of a car, the rest of the world had caught up with me. At the end of 2017, the Southbank Centre staged a special interactive exhibition to celebrate the group. I brought my husband – a man who has music built into his bones, who has the same love, respect and enthusiasm for Bauhaus as Beyoncé. He didn't think of ABBA as a joke, or a siren call to the least proficient dancers at the end of a wedding. He knows they are some of the greatest and most influential pop artists of the twentieth century.

I think he was expecting a display of nerdiness from his wife. He thought I might obnoxiously mention the name of some less well-known album tracks, or ask irritating questions that are really statements, actually, about their solo careers. He didn't realise that I was going to walk around the exhibition weeping for my lost loves, overcome by the prospect of sharing my special Swedes with some fans who were, frankly, a bit casual. (One woman was confused by a room that had been designed to replicate the set of the video for 'One Of Us', a devastating song about the end of Agnetha and Björn's relationship, which shows Agnetha seemingly moving out of the family home and decorating her new flat. The woman pointed to a prop box of kitchen equipment, and asked the guide, 'Were these the actual pots and pans that ABBA used?' At this point the guide was so frustrated by the woman and her endless questions that she sighed and simply said, 'Yes. These were Agnetha's real pans.')

ABBA came into my life at a time when I desperately needed friends of my own choosing. I was being badly bullied at school (or, as the old joke goes, I was being very efficiently and effectively bullied) and I didn't know where to find support. My sisters were too close to home, in every sense, so I ended up making distant pop stars into imaginary friends. In my head, I shared my biggest dreams and scariest secrets with the band, dreaming of the conversations we'd have, going on glamorous trips to New York and Hollywood, as the family Peugeot pulled into Toddington Services. Then Livvy would lay her head on my lap, or Grace would smile and point out our favourite sign, the giant warehouse that was available 'TO LET', and bisected by a structural beam, forcing us to guffaw, as only under-tens can, at the idea that someone was renting out their enormous toilet. And I'd be glad to be back, delighted that I could dream about being sophisticated, and then celebrate the silly with my sisters in real life.

Those car journeys had allowed me to imagine ABBA as my emergency future family, and they had allowed me to escape from the difficulties of being a big sister, a member of a unit that sometimes felt slightly suffocating. They helped me to hope, and their words showed me a new way of making sense of the world. I had a new, special world to explore, and a degree of emotional privacy for the very first time.

Yet I knew my sisters were experiencing something similar. We could share the cramped space, while experiencing something that belonged to us individually. Singing in the car gave us all space to dream. We had the chance to be together, but we could reconcile our unavoidable physical closeness with the fact that these strange and lovely songs were prompting us to gaze out of the window and make sense of the world on our own terms. Those songs are our legacy. To this day, I know we all hold a magic key. The rhythm of those words have their own special code. I can start a call-and-response with any of my sisters, across a crowded room, by mouthing the first line of 'Take a Chance on Me'. Sometimes I'll know exactly what they're thinking, and sometimes I'll catch a glimpse of their expression and understand that some part of them will always be completely unknowable, even though we're all made of the very same stuff.

August 2011: The Band Gets Back Together

Like ABBA, our band had been broken up for some time, but that didn't stop the swirl of reunion rumours. My sisters and I rarely travelled together any more. Occasionally Grace, the only driver in the family, would give me a lift in her silver Honda, a haven of books on tape and blossoming Magic Trees. After driving past the dealership on his way to work, Dad purchased a Jaguar on a whim and would sometimes offer to drive us short distances so that we might experience the heated seats, and resultant soggy bottoms on summer days. But it had been a long, long time since I'd been in a car with all of my sisters, ridden with my ride-or-dies. We were all scattered across the country. The only sister who still lived at home was Livvy, and she often complained that she saw Mum and Dad less than the rest of us, as they'd just become giddily, feverishly obsessed with amateur dramatics.

Then our parents announced that they had rented a place in the South of France over August, and perhaps we could all fly down for a few days, once they'd arrived. They were planning a leisurely, romantic drive through the countryside, allowing them to spend some time together, now that their children had all, more or less, left home.

So one day in early August, my parents set off for the ferry terminal. In two separate cars. Because their spoiled, lazy, useless children hadn't got it together and made independent arrangements, so they were forced to ferry us to the ferry, and beyond. We were all significantly wider and heavier than we had been during our last trip, and only marginally less likely to wet ourselves.

As their nest emptied out, my parents had ditched the Previa – the eight-seater made for Catholic families and nascent boy bands – and had acquired a Prius, the smug A-lister's car of choice, and a Corsa, the must-have vehicle for anyone who prioritises the comfort of the shopping in the boot over that of their passengers. The Prius had air conditioning, and was a much more comfortable experience for anyone who owned knees. But it had the distinct disadvantage of being driven by my father. Dad drives as though every single other motorist on the road has deliberately missold him PPI. He truly believes everyone else has got into their cars to taunt and inconvenience him. Mum has her faults too. Her talent for navigation is overshadowed by her enthusiasm for it, but at least she has some chill. Being in cars with my parents is a little bit like being in *The Fast and the Furious.* Dad is a Hulk-smashing Vin Diesel, and Mum is the British woman who gets thrown from an exploding car, dusts herself off and says, 'Well, there goes my road atlas.' The experience is compounded by Dad's occasional but severe Continental anxiety, when he turns around and shouts at his passengers, 'Don't forget, remind me to drive on *the wrong side of the road.*'

So our holiday mood was imbued with something of a war-zone sensibility. My sisters and I had to pick a parent, and most horrifyingly of all, help with the navigation, Dad having decided quite early on that the sat nav lady was Sybil to his Basil Fawlty. There were several crises. We got stuck behind a toll booth barrier, and my GCSE French was more suited to a game of Articulate than solving a practical problem. ('The car, she cannot take our money, we would like to use the card of the bank for our forward moving.') We accidentally drove through what I now realise was some kind of archaeological dig. Dad was ostensibly upset about the car's suspension, but I suspect this was really a nervousness about his bladder. We stopped for a picnic and ended up giving about sixty euros to an extremely persistent beggar, believing he was a car park attendant. We traumatised Mum by playing some Jay-Z deep cuts ('*What* did that man just say?') and got carsick texting each other with news of new and inventive parental curses. There was no ABBA, no singing, and no daydreaming out of the window. I wasn't sure why I'd come.

Then, on the outskirts of Caen, a tiny miracle happened. We saw the sign we had been waiting for. A grey, shuttered concrete square of a building with bold red signage. 'SEXY SHOP' it proclaimed, in a font that was slightly too swollen to be Comic Sans. I was aware of a strange, low honking – it was a noise I had never heard before, and I was making it. Figuratively and literally, I nearly died. Bending at the waist, I leaned all the way out of the window to take a picture of the 'SEXY SHOP', laughing so hard that I almost dropped my phone. As I leaned I heard gales of laughter from the car behind me. 'Quick, tell Daisy! Tell her to take a pic . . . SHE'S DOING IT, SHE'S DOING IT!' yelled Grace, as she noticed my torso protruding from the passenger window. I have never felt sillier, or more understood. I was consumed by hilarious, ridiculous, unsexy love for the Sexy Shop, and for my fierce, fabulous, daft sisters.

CHAPTER THIRTEEN
Surrogate Sisters and Women at Work

I have always been suspicious of any employer who boasts about the 'family atmosphere' of their workplace. If someone tells you that if you work for them, you'll be 'part of the family', it means that you'll be expected to share your stationery, you will be told to stop squabbling over the office thermostat, and that other people will eat your lunch if you're not looking. (Or it means that you're now in the Mafia.) The *hell* of most offices is that you do have a new family, you don't get to choose any of them and you have to fight for every square centimetre of personal space. However, the enforced intimacy means that most of the women I know, myself included, have acquired a lot of surrogate sisters over the course of their professional lives.

When I was twenty-three, and an intern at *Bliss* magazine, I looked up one day and realised I'd suddenly picked up twelve brand new sisters without realising. I wasn't thrilled, initially. I already had plenty of sisters, and those relationships were consuming and difficult without adding more to the pile. But I realised that the way I felt about Leslie, Angeli, Louise, Fatima, Zoe, Lydia, Frankie, Nadine, Abby, Jo, Nic and Vicky wasn't purely professional. I liked their company. I respected their work. But when I was with them, I felt as though I belonged to them entirely, in a way I'd never experienced with anyone beyond my family. Angeli didn't just praise my work – she was an entire cheer squad for it, and I felt raised up by her constant kindness. When I met Fatima the fashion editor, I felt slightly shy – not just because she is one of the most beautiful people I'd ever beheld, but because I'd seen *The Devil Wears Prada* and I was convinced she would be repulsed by my Primark pussy bow jumper and French Connection clearance skirt – but she was endlessly sweet, never sneery. 'You're always so well put together,' she murmured, as I shuffled past her desk. It was the greatest compliment from the cool big sister I'd never had. I walked on air for a week.

Then there was Zoe. I didn't fully understand my relationship with Zoe until I watched the Will Ferrell film, *Step Brothers*. Ferrell and John C. Reilly play adult men who refuse to move out of their family homes. They're brought together when their parents fall in love, and they hate each other on sight – until that hatred metamorphoses to ride or die friendship. It's a love story for the ages. Zoe thought I was posh, weird, earnest and *much* too enthusiastic. I thought Zoe was standoffish, pretentious and chilly. On my very first day of work, we were sent to a film premiere together (*Angus, Thongs and Perfect Snogging*). For the first time in my life, I discovered how it felt to be the little sister, the one whose very existence infuriates the person who is supposed to be looking after you. Zoe narrated the celebrity entrances – 'Oh, thingy from *Hollyoaks* just walked in, with that model who does the water – NO! DON'T LOOK! STOP LOOKING! I

FORBID YOU TO LOOK!' I went home immediately afterwards because I was terrified of going to the afterparty and disgracing myself at the chocolate fountain.

I would like to tell you that slowly we learned to trust each other, and our mutual admiration turned to intimacy. Here is what really happened. We went to a very odd Sugababes album party launch in a clothes shop (line up: Keisha, Heidi, Amelle). We drank until there was no more champagne left. Our inhibitions dissolved, we discovered that we were equally nerdy, bitchy and dazzled by our access to this rarefied world where we could dine nightly on teeny tiny hamburgers. Then I went home to my boyfriend in Chiswick, where I went to bed and got up in the middle of the night while still asleep. Instead of turning left and going to the bathroom, I turned right, pulled out his desk drawer and sleep weed all over a stack of very expensive textbooks that he had bought for his Economics course.

He was not pleased. The next morning, I left the house convinced that when I returned I would be boyfriendless, and without anywhere to live. Zoe saw my face and assumed someone I loved had died in the night. She made me a cup of tea. As a Catholic, I was desperate to confess my sins to someone – and Zoe made the most appreciative audience I could have hoped for. She still describes that time as 'the day we took our relationship to the next level'. I fixed things with the boyfriend, through the medium of heartfelt apologies and expensive steak. And I had a new sibling. Because when someone tells you that they have pissed in a drawer by accident, you can only cut them out of your life completely or see the funny side and love them forever.

When friends seem like sisters, you start to grant each other an enormous amount of freedom. You can be outrageous and unfiltered when you're around each other. You feel protected by your intimacy and cocooned by it. The relationship can become as fractious and unmanageable as relationships with biological sisters, too. I've been jealous of Zoe's friends, and boyfriends. I've given her advice impatiently, and been unsupportive, mistakenly thinking that I don't just know her well, but better than she knows herself. We spent eight hours a day, five days a week sitting next to each other for four years. Throughout, we behaved like eight-year-olds sharing a bedroom. Then my twin left our cosy, glittery womb. Zoe got a job on a different magazine, where she had more responsibility and more money. Everyone at *Bliss* was thrilled for her. I would have been happier if I'd been told that both my legs were being amputated. In fact Zoe could have had my legs, if she'd only stay. Of course, I was deeply jealous of the opportunity that lay before her, and the fact that her talents had been recognised. But I was also struggling with the sensation of being left behind and abandoned. I didn't know who I was at work without Zoe beside me.

Where there is pain, there is growth. Zoe had shown courage. She'd left the comfort zone we'd been curating together. I truly hate being brave, but she forced me to try, and I left *Bliss* nine months after she did. Together, we'd constantly complained about work. (That's what sisters do – and it's startling how quickly you start to take the tiny hamburgers for granted.) But when I had to think for myself, I discovered that I was startlingly ambitious – and that I could do so much work alone that I didn't have time to complain.

Zoe and I have both flown in different directions – but we really have flown. Zoe now lives in LA, and I think she's the happiest that she's ever been. I believe neither of us would have worked out how to have the careers or lives we adore if we hadn't learned so much from loving each other so hard, or been surrounded by sweet, sisterly women who raised us and raised us up. She's still my dear, darling friend, and we're always really happy to hear from each other – and at points I think our friendship was too intense to continue in the *Bliss* bubble. We had to grow up and move on. Still, sometimes I think about quiet Friday afternoons, sneakily drinking warm white wine at our desks, flicking stale cupcake crumbs at each other, trying on clothes meant for teenagers in the back boardroom, listening to hip hop, writing each other's dating profiles, giggling and bitching and poking each other, and I want to weep. We were each other's surrogate kid sisters, and I had more fun with her than I've ever had with anyone else. I miss her very much.

However, I know there will be more surrogate sisters, and other Big Loves. I used to worry that I have already experienced much more than my fair share of love in my lifetime, and it's only a matter of time before I encounter a biblical drought. But I fall in love with new sisters all the time. At festivals, in book clubs, swimming in the local tidal pool, the light will change, I'll look at my nice new friend and think, 'You could have my kidney, if you wanted it.' Feelings fluctuate, and I think we're living through a thrilling and bewildering new era of female friendship. It's easier than it's ever been to stay in touch with old friends, if you want to. It's also easier than ever to convert your casual coffee shop friendship into something more meaningful – if swapping numbers is a bit intense, you can follow each other on social media. We're changing jobs and moving house much more than previous generations, and this means that maintaining intimate friendships is hard. But I think it means we've got a bigger group to choose from, and a better chance of finding our spiritual sisters. Some of them are for life, and some of them are for the duration of a temp job, or just a sunny afternoon. But you will know them by the sense of freedom you feel when you're with them.

Lauren

As an engagement present, I got Grace a cake stand. In return, she found me a new best friend.

I was on my way back from trying on bridesmaids' dresses, and tweeted my glee, because we'd all chosen our outfits within about half an hour and managed to knock off early for Bloody Marys. One of my followers, Dan, had replied to tweet. 'Hey @laurenbravo, do you know this girl? She sounds EXACTLY like you!'

I looked at Lauren's profile. She had significantly more followers than me, and she was a columnist and a food writer for Channel 4. I immediately felt jealous. I didn't know who this girl was, but she was clearly extremely successful, she was much prettier than me, and she probably had a perfect life, boyfriend, north London townhouse and one of those coffee makers that actually grinds the beans. Still, I was intrigued. Her tweets were funny, and we seemed to share the same great loves – Amy Winehouse and custard. Cautiously, I followed.

A few months later, I met Lauren at a Twitter gathering, arranged by our friend Ashley. She remembered about the bridesmaids' dresses, and asked me about the wedding, so I could fill her in. All of the dresses were fine, I was frightened that I wouldn't be able to get into mine because I'd recently developed a chronic Morrisons quiche habit, Grace seemed pretty chilled, the canapes were chosen and they'd just booked a caller for a barn dance. I learned about Lauren. Her boyfriend was called Matt, and they'd met on My Single Friend. She lived with her old university friends between Finsbury Park and Wood Green, a street away from a deli that made the best hummus in the world. And her dad was a journalist too – he was the editor of the *Herald*, a Christian newspaper I had grown up seeing in church. *That* was when I felt like Eliot touching fingers with E.T. We'd been brought up like sisters, even if we didn't know it. We were raised by people who believed in God, giggling and Noel Streatfeild. We wanted to be Nora Ephron and Joan Didion, but we couldn't help but talk like Enid Blyton. We'd go to church with eye-rolling resignation, and intentions of parental appeasement, but we still knew our Catechism back to front when none of our other friends knew what the Catechism was. Lauren is the same age as Grace, and it seemed as though Grace had performed an act of premarital magic. She didn't want me to feel left behind, so she set up the circumstances that led me to a brand new friend.

We do look similar – in some lights, in some pictures, more similar than anyone else in my family. At my wedding, Lauren was repeatedly mistaken for one of my sisters, even though she wasn't wearing a bridesmaid's dress. I appreciate that as a white, blonde woman, it's very easy to find people who look like me – and I'd argue that it would be a great benefit to the world if we could turn on the TV or go to the cinema and see more women who aren't white or blonde. Still, there's something magical about being able to see yourself in your friend's face, and marvel at the fact that even though you were brought together by a combination of chance and luck, something bigger seems to be linking you to them.

I'd like to think that my relationship with Lauren has made me a kinder, better big sister. Friends are different from sisters, and the rules for maintaining friendship are more rigid. There comes a point where you can't assume your presence in each other's lives, you can only appreciate it. Because Lauren came into my life without much context, I can't judge her from old stories, memories and anecdotes. I have to take her at face value. As our friendship developed, I started to think that I could relate to my sisters better if we did it too – and that I needed to start concentrating on who they are, not who they had been.

I can be vulnerable with Lauren in a way that I can't with my sisters, although I think my relationship with her has forced me to become more honest with them. She's helped me to realise that I'm not helping my sisters when I hold back. When I share my fears and failures with them, I'm showing them that no one is perfect, and that it's OK to be frightened.

I think that almost all women go through a point in their teens or twenties where they say, 'Girls are *so* bitchy, I get on much better with boys.' And it's obnoxious and infuriating, but entirely understandable. 'Boys' girl' is one of the intriguing identities we try on for size, along with 'girl who always wears red lipstick and a Breton', 'girl who always stands at the front at gigs' and 'girl who loves gin and talks about buying a record player'. Because ultimately, that's what being a boys' girl is all about. It's a two-dimensional, limiting label that we seek because we feel insecure – wanting only to be fancied from a safe distance by boys who are frightened of ruining the friendship.

Admittedly I went through a brief but tedious phase of having very contrived connections with friends-who-were-boys, in which I behaved like a bellend. Now, I have a few man pals and I love and appreciate them very much. But those friendships lack depth, and I don't think it's the men's fault. It's how I'm wired. Other than my husband, my deepest relationships are with girls and women, and I think it's because I feel as though most of the women I meet could be my sisters. I have the same urge to bond with them, protect them, worry about them, shower them with tampons and £20 notes for emergency taxis, send them *Simpsons* gifs, and let them rest their head in my laps during long car journeys.

It's such a magnificent, difficult, infuriating and interesting time to be a woman. Every day something horrible happens that might not impact me directly and immediately, but will certainly affect a woman I love, or a woman they love. But we're getting angry together, and that anger has an energy. If someone else is missing out or getting hurt, we're not going to the ball – we're getting pissed off and fighting for each other together.

Women dazzle me every day. I never stop feeling stunned by the wit, talent, energy, creativity and tenacity I'm surrounded by, thanks to the women in my life. We've all grown up hearing some confusing messages. We can have it all and do everything! Every single one of us can, and must, be exceptional! While I am always longing for the comeback of the lady slacker, every single woman I know seems deeply driven. Yet womanhood is fraught with a sort of gallows humour. We're all constantly trying to break out of patriarchy prison while making each other laugh, because womanhood would be utterly miserable if you didn't devote lots of energy to finding the fun and making the job a game.

Being a sister has made me want to fight *for* women, even if I'm occasionally filled with an urge to fight with them too. There is no part of feminism that makes it mandatory for us all to like each other. Women aren't inherently kinder or more noble than men. We can all be absolute dicks to each other, on occasion. That's equality. However, I am a girls' girl to my core. This doesn't make me a better feminist, or a better person. It has nothing to do with my predilection for sparkly phone cases, my addiction to Kate Spade or the fact that if I were to take a deep breath and calculate exactly how much money I've spent on perfume I'd come up with a sum large enough to buy a second-hand family car.

There's something about being among a group of women that makes me feel intuitive and understood. My relationships with women have been the great big love affairs of my life, slow-burning, cautiously forged connections that begin with compliments and coffee, and end in three-bottle lunches, WhatsApp conversations that last for months and years, borrowed shoes, swapped books and shared pin numbers. I think we're so keenly attuned to the fact that we can feel so strong and so vulnerable in the same moment that we celebrate each other's strengths and respect the vulnerabilities. We sense our sisters, and we find gangs within our families, and families within our gangs.

I think this is a golden era for female friendships. It's like dating. We don't live in one place, we don't stay in one job, and we're meeting more people than ever – so if you feel as though you haven't met your kindred spirit at school or university, she might come into your life in your thirties, forties or beyond. The one thing that makes me endlessly optimistic about life and women is that I know I share a sense of sisterhood with women I have yet to meet. These relationships can be intense, painful and complicated, but they enhance my life. I've been friends with women who have hurt me horribly, but that doesn't stop me from being a hopeless friendship romantic. Reaching out and asking for friendship can feel as terrifying as sticking your hand in an open fire, but if you take the leap, you might meet a Lauren.

Lauren facts

- ○ My first proper 'date' with Lauren was a spanking workshop held in a high-end sex shop, hosted by three people who used to be in *Made in Chelsea*. I think we both went because it was free. We were given goody bags that contained flat, wide, wooden sticks, each retailing at £49.95.

- ○ Lauren would be my *Desert Island Discs* luxury, because she would be able to make the world's most delicious salad out of coconut and palm leaves. She's better at eating than anyone I know, she has a psychic sense for discovering the very best brunch places in London, and she's the only person apart from Ottolenghi who can actually use pomegranate molasses. But she would never judge me for eating Super Noodles when I'm hungover.

- ○ Whenever I meet someone who knows of Lauren and her work, they immediately ask me to tell them Lauren's haircare 'secrets'. (Her hair is long, shiny and golden, like the platonic ideal of a mermaid's.)

- ○ We once planned a picnic in which we read out our favourite extracts of *Bridget Jones' Diary*. We ate M&S

salmon pinwheels and Dairy Milk, washed down with
Chardonnay, to replicate the meal Bridget eats with her
best friends Shaz and Jude.

✪ At the time of writing, Lauren is searching for the
perfect yellow sundress. If you think you have seen it,
please get in touch.

CHAPTER FOURTEEN
Comedy and Drama

Every family has its own mythology, and translating that mythology is tricky. In-jokes breed in-jokes, stories of school plays and supermarket tantrums become engraved on our hearts, and there's a risk of becoming blind to your collective banality. Deep down, we all believe that we're unique and hilarious, when we're all exactly the same in a slightly different way, and in some lights, probably quite boring. This is how I interpret the *Anna Karenina* principle – that happy families are all alike, whereas every unhappy family is unhappy in its own way. Happy families replicate each other's rhythms. There is a finite number of ways that a group can function successfully. We focus on the tiny differences, and we seek out moments of specialness. This is very human. Yet overall, successful units tend to follow convention.

I think this is partly because the family is such a visible emblem of unity. It's really difficult to be wholly independent of convention, when you've got to make sure that everyone is getting on. If you've got a parent who regularly took you out of school to tour a series of ashrams, or decided to self-actualise by bringing you up in a Scottish bothy with no electricity, I would guess that there were moments when you thought it might be nice to live with the sort of family that ate the same meal at the same time every Friday night, washed down with instant gravy.

At times in my teens, I cursed my family for being so normal and boring. In my thirties, I realise that being bored by your family is a great luxury. We're all built to endure dull days, because there are so many of them. While I fantasised about bohemia in Bloomsbury, or being the child of millionaire punks and life in a Manhattan loft, I could only do so because I knew I was very loved, and that I would always have a supply of clean knickers.

Being part of a big family was my only hallmark of specialness – the only element of my home life that seemed a little bit less conventional than my school friends' lives. The way the unit exists in my imagination has been heavily filtered and Photoshopped. I've definitely passed anecdotes off as my own, before realising they really belong to *The Waltons*. Or *The Simpsons*. For a long time, I labelled us as a funny family, without considering the fact that we're all so blessed with stimulus that any family is funny when there are enough of you to form a decently sized improv troupe.

I've become wary of saying my sisters are especially witty, because we're probably just normally funny. We're a typical example of what happens when you bring a gang of women together with a shared past, and you've all known each other at everyone's silliest stage. It's gloriously disinhibiting. But when I'm with them, I realise that there is so much freedom in funniness. It's *pure*. At Christmas, at Easter, in the pub, or sitting around the kitchen table, we push each other further and further, with no agenda beyond trying to make each other laugh past the point of pain. We play much more nicely now than we ever did when we were little.

Still, the best thing about growing up with girls is that it never, ever entered my head that women couldn't be funny. Women were the ones making me laugh all day long. Every Friday, I'd watch *Have I Got News for You* and try to understand why a load of middle-aged men could bring down the house by saying things like, 'Ah, the thing about Michael Heseltine is that he'd have a great cabinet if only he could find a decent carpenter! Ho ho ho!' My sisters were ten thousand times funnier, and weirder – and while I'm pretty sure that BBC1 would never make room on their schedule for a satirical gag about how Maddy nearly shat herself during her SATS by eating three packets of sugar-free Polos in twenty minutes, I realised my sisters made me laugh more than most professional comedians because they had a sense of humour about *themselves*.

A very, very funny woman lived in our house. Not in a corporeal sense, but she was referred to and celebrated so often that she functioned as a kind of auxiliary aunt, and there was a little bit of life advice wrapped up in every line that she spoke to us, even though we were usually hearing it third hand. My parents were both Victoria Wood super fans. I hung out with Victoria every time I went to the toilet. There wasn't a loo in the house that didn't have a book of her scripts, nestled between the collection of vintage *Reader's Digest*. Dad would constantly prompt us with different lines at dinner. My sisters and I still know every single word of Julie Walters' Pie Crust Players monologue, as she gives notes for the world's worst amateur production of *Hamlet*.

(Whenever anyone was dreading a task that seemed particularly dull, dismal or heavy, the rest of us would unhelpfully chorus, 'It may be *Hamlet*, but it's got to be fun, fun, fun!')

Every single one of us explored theatre and drama to some degree, and I think that we have Victoria to thank. More importantly, we all realised that we could have a voice, and that being funny is one of the best ways of being heard. Being exposed to her words shaped us all and made us realise that we could get the world to pay attention to what we had to say, as long as we looked for the laugh. Victoria Wood also constantly cast brilliant women to bring her words to life. She'd built a world that was made for my sisters and me. It was exacting, but democratic. Wit would earn you a place at the table, but that place wasn't contingent on anything but your ability to be funny and clever. It didn't matter how you looked or how old you were. Comedy brought my sisters and me together, and I stopped being a status-obsessed, bitchy big sister as soon as I realised that we were funnier when we acted like equals.

Every drama student knows that the first rule of improvisation is that you never say no. You're given an idea, a scenario or a proposition, and you respond with a 'yes, and . . .' My sisters and I grew up improvising, without fully understanding what we were doing. My friend Kit is in an improv troup, and she explained to me that you can only be funny when you have total trust in each other. 'You can't be selfish; you have to cooperate, and bring equal amounts of energy and enthusiasm to the table. It's not fair to carry or be carried, or rather, you can take turns to carry each other, but you know that it's best when you're all daring each other to do better. No one is supposed to be a star; it's about combining talents and lifting each other up.'

On occasion, my sisters and I can all be vicious, venal, petty, selfish, exploitative, manipulative and cruel with each other. Yet, when we're making each other laugh, we somehow swerve our worst tendencies. Even when we're making fun of each other, I think we all believe that if our first goal is funniness, we can survive some accidental meanness. And we've worked out a way of being quite cruel about ourselves, while protecting ourselves. After all, if someone is going to make fun of you for the sake of a joke, it's better to jump in and do it yourself, and then *you* get the laugh.

Do you want to know a secret? I believe women are funnier than men. Not for reasons that have anything to do with biology, but because we're all socialised to be thinking and worrying about seventeen things at any given time. Our brains are forced to hold and process huge amounts of disparate information, and so we're used to spotting the silliness, the outliers, the ludicrous contradictions. I also think that we have to see the funny side, as a form of survival. Womanhood is an endless and hilarious black comedy, and our body and our lives are constantly conspiring to play tricks on us. If you're not sure what I mean, come back to me when you've used your bare hands to pull out a thick black hair that has grown out of the middle of your chin in the time it takes you to get to work and glance in a mirror. Seriously, *how* can that happen? The only thing that would make my adult hair situation make any sense would be finding out that tiny people live in my jaw, and they're always trying to escape by throwing out guide ropes and attempting to abseil out of my face.

There are plenty of funny women who should be all over our TVs and radios, and they aren't. The ones that are constantly get asked, 'What's it like being a woman in comedy?' and to their eternal credit, almost no one ever responds with: 'Dunno. What's it like to be a journalist who is so shite and lacking in imagination that they can't think of a better question than "How do you do that job with boobs?"' When we talk about women in comedy as though they are freaks, like Samuel Johnson's hypothetical upright dogs, we're forgetting the first rule of improv. A funny woman is a 'yes, and?' type. When we tell jokes together, we're sharpening our strongest survival tool. So much of being a woman is horrible unless you're prepared to find it hilarious, and when you can laugh at life, you stop being scared. My sisters taught me that nothing is ever as bad as it seems if you can get a gag out of it, and that when we're funny together, we raise each other up. If we can all laugh together, we can all lift each other. Most importantly, when we're funny, we're noisy. Laughter gets us heard. Even if we don't want to tell the joke, we can boost the women who do by showing our appreciation. Remember, the idea that women *aren't* funny is perpetuated by men who don't want people to know what's genuinely hilarious, because it would prevent them from building careers on snarky non-jokes about Michael Heseltine.

For years, comedy was the only thing that any of us could agree on. Beth was a freak, and looked like a Blink 182 groupie who had got bored during a gig, wandered off and fallen into the back of a van bound for the *Antiques Roadshow*.

Grace was also a freak, because she actually liked school, and vegetables, and genuinely thought she was going to marry Legolas from *Lord of the Rings,* even though she denied it and burst into furious tears every time I introduced her to people as 'my loser sister who is in love with an imaginary gnome'. And I was a freak who didn't know the difference between an elf and a gnome, no matter how many times my horribly condescending boyfriend told me. Livvy, Maddy and Dotty had found a pocket of serenity and unity, bonding over a Pokémon called Jigglypuff who Dotty solemnly described to me as 'a flying wanker'. But the adolescent portion of the family were furious individualists who were committed to writing nightly, inky diary entries about how misunderstood they were, and how their sisters were probably aliens, and so different and purposefully perverse that we couldn't possibly share the same DNA.

Then we discovered *Father Ted.*

Father Ted took our utter weirdness, the one big, mad, slightly shameful thing we had in common, and made jokes about it. But the jokes weren't mean – they had kindness and compassion at their very core. There was nothing cruel or sneery about it – it simply held up a mirror and said, 'Look! See how totally bizarre this is!' Perhaps as importantly, it made us all feel as though other people understood us. We could talk to our friends and say, 'I know you think it's odd that we can never hang out on a Sunday, but this is what we do all morning.' Perhaps ironically, it made us realise that nothing is sacred. There is nothing in the world that can't be funny. But if you're going to send it up successfully, you can't get away with it unless it's really fucking funny.

It was the first time we'd seen anything that seemed to be made for us, and this was made for all of us. Being fans of the programme made us feel grown up, but the jokes were exhilaratingly childish. For all of us, it was dizzying and thrilling that someone else knew how it felt to be Catholic – that there was another world, albeit a fictional one, where it was normal for a busload of very intense nuns to turn up at your house and expect you to provide a sufficient (that is, unlimited) supply of biscuits. Thanks to *Father Ted*, we were all in a special club.

Obviously, the Catholic Church isn't famous for having a big sense of humour about itself, but we quickly cottoned on to the fact that being pompous and pretentious is the fastest way to be made fun of. It was a masterclass in status – it's easier to maintain your identity when you're not precious about it. As we borrowed shamelessly from the show, we discovered that we did have a sense of humour about ourselves. We learned that life is so much more fun when you can appreciate what other people find strange and hilarious about you – and that the funnier you feel, the more resilient you become.

You can't be a good friend and sister and maintain your ego at the same time. It's imperative to find a balance between being kind, supportive and uplifting, and *utterly merciless*. As women, we're told two irritating and conflicting things. Officially, we're supposed to embrace the act of self-promotion. We must stop being self-deprecating and putting ourselves down if we're ever going to achieve great things, otherwise we're not leaning in enough and it's all our fault that most boardrooms contain fewer women than men named

Gary. However, it is strongly implied that any displays of unironic pride or self-love will lead to mockery and public shaming, and tabloid think pieces in which young women are castigated by unkempt, overconfident middle-aged men who think we're all livetweeting our boob jobs as a display of confidence.

However, my sisters have taught me that self-deprecation has many shades and flavours. When I'm with my girls, I need to be prepared to be the butt of every joke I tell, for the sake of survival. If I don't say it, they'll beat me to it. Like Nora Ephron, I'm extremely possessive of *my* stories, *my* banana skins. However, you need to like yourself at least a little in order to tell a joke that doesn't work in your favour, otherwise the story sounds sad, not funny. Making people laugh while making fun of yourself requires self-esteem and a cast iron emotional constitution. Humans are hilarious, and it's imperative that we see our funny sides. How can I miss them, when I'm surrounded by them? We reflect each other's personalities like funfair mirrors, and their faults and foibles are magnified by mine. If I'm going to be cruel about Dotty's grumpiness or Maddy's extreme mood swings, I have to admit that it takes one to know one. When Livvy was younger and bragged about kissing boys and going to clubs, I knew that I couldn't mock her without making fun of myself and admitting that I was every bit as obnoxious about my exploits when I was a teenager.

Developing a sense of humour about myself has been my most useful survival tool for getting through the business of being a woman. I don't want to use jokes as a defensive shield, but I do think it's a way of acknowledging my vulnerability while making it very clear that I'm not too fragile to cope with life's major exasperations. I've held my nerve during contract negotiations by using an emotional muscle I first started to flex when Beth was cheating at Guess Who? When I've been trolled by internet strangers, I've laughed and thought, 'You'll have to do better than that. Grace could think of much more vicious things to call me when she was five years old.' There is a toughness and tenderness to sisterhood, and I think that much of our meanness is borne out of an urge to protect and defend. We can't always be there to protect each other, but we can ensure that we're schooled in sticking up for ourselves. Also, we want to be sure that no one in the world would ever be meaner or crueller to our sisters than we're capable of being, so we make sure the bar is set quite high.

Of course, most of us are too evolved to even question the funniness of women, or to entertain any suggestion that we're the least witty sex. But it's worth wondering why the idea persists, and asking why we're still not seeing women in comedy getting the opportunities that they deserve, when men are still being invited onto prime-time TV to do a substandard Trump impression. There are obvious answers – the workings of the entertainment industry are, in places, more sexist and outdated than a Miss Crinoline competition. The comedian and writer Deborah Frances-White once compared the experience of being a lone woman on a panel show with being at an extremely stressful, televised job interview, while the men – regular guests who know the format well – can relax, as if they're spending the afternoon in the pub.

But at a fundamental level, I think there's a bigger reason why women 'aren't funny' – we've been encouraged to hide our funniness, because we've been made to believe it exemplifies every part of us that isn't feminine. You can't tell a joke if you feel as though you should be quiet and speak when you're spoken to. You can't swear, or make fun of people, because it isn't 'nice'. You can't draw attention to your physicality in case people notice that you're not being dainty. One of my favourite comedians, Joe Wilkinson, almost always performs in the same outfit, a dark brown suit and a stripy tie. He's got an enormous bushy beard, and his general aesthetic is that of a 1970s geography teacher. I'm assuming that he has several identical suits that he wears on rotation, but his slightly unkempt look is rarely remarked upon. It's simply a uniform. But if a female comedian wore exactly the same outfit for every public appearance and stopped shaving, people wouldn't talk about any of her jokes. People would assume that *was* the joke.

I have deep love and respect for every woman in comedy, because they must have been able to find a voice in their head and argue it out with their inner parent, priest or the elderly aunt who made them feel that nice girls don't pull silly faces, or show off. These are the women who give us so many modes of being, who give us evidence that if you've got an urge to show off, instead of shoving it away and feeling ashamed of it, you can work at it, practise it, and do something brilliant. These women show us how to find the power in feeling powerless – by laughing at it. Even though I don't know these women, they make me feel as good, as loved and as connected as my sisters do. With all my heart, I urge you to seek out the work of Roisin Conaty, Helen Lederer, Sara Pascoe, Cariad Lloyd, Jayde Adams, Deborah Frances-White, Sofie Hagen, Lolly Adefope, Tara Flynn, Alison Spittle, Tessa Coates, Stevie Martin, Sharon Horgan, Isy Suttie, Bridget Christie and Luisa Omielan – and that is the tiniest, chilliest tip of the iceberg. There's a wealth of wonderful work and words out there, and I'm speaking as someone who would always rather be laughing than doing anything else, including having sex, sleeping and eating.

Being a woman would be a miserable, constant catastrophe if we couldn't find the funny side. We will never run out of material. My sisters can find the jokes in tampons and traffic jams. I've had haircuts that reduced me to tears, and then cried all over again, with laughter, while Beth does a bad impression of me as Ronald McDonald. They can even make the jokes in Christmas crackers sound funny. So much of womanhood seems tragic to the point of being Shakespearean. We struggle through huge losses, tiny disappointments, running uphill and getting let down – but because we keep laughing, we can keep trying. It might feel like *Hamlet*, but it's got to be fun, fun, fun!

Maddy

Maddy's hair, they say, is full of secrets. Ever since she's been allowed to be in charge of it, she's worn it in the same way. It's thick and dark, and she keeps it long, coiling it and pinning it to the top of her head, a shiny, full plume of Elnett. To see Maddy without her hair up would be like looking at a picture of Abraham Lincoln in which he was not wearing a stovepipe hat. Maddy and I both have intensely loving and complicated feelings for the dead singer Amy Winehouse. I reckon Maddy is paying tribute to Amy every time she does her hair.

When you're fifth in the family, I think it's important to feel as though you're in charge of something, and that's why Maddy's approach to barnet management borders on the baroque. Like every one of my sisters, and possibly every human being that's ever been born, I think Maddy longs to be taken a little bit more seriously. However, Maddy seems to have appropriated her life philosophy from a drama student's favourite terrible tattoo. Everything is either comedy or tragedy. Life is terrible, but also hilarious. And if you have to pick a side on which everything must fall, you should always choose hilarity.

As Maddy's big sister, it was easy to see her as a leader. She and Dotty were part of a gang, with two other little girls, and Maddy seemed to be the one whose voice carried, who had all the ideas. 'Let's pretend the garage is haunted!' 'Let's make a fort with a clothes horse!' 'Let's get our Barbies and do a photo shoot!' (In the pre-digital era, the latter was a source of constant frustration for our poor father, who would regularly spend twenty or thirty quid developing what he believed to be holiday photos, only to get back rolls and rolls of Barbies in the garden wearing cut-up curtains.)

However, when Maddy was in her teens, I had the chance to get to know her better. I was twenty-three, I'd been fired from my first ever grown-up job and I'd moved back in with my parents. I worked at the same call centre that had employed me before I went to university. I felt like a teenager again. It seemed as though my life was sliding backwards, out of my grasp. Everything I'd worked so hard at when I'd been Maddy's age was rendered completely pointless.

When I'd gone to university, four years before I came back, Maddy was eleven and I hadn't known how to talk to her. We were a little bit shy of each other, and I think we found each other slightly boring. Being at opposite ends of the family polarised us, and we weren't sure that we could have any common ground. However, fifteen-year-old Maddy was a brilliant brand new mate. We'd talk to each other after dinner, and sometimes we'd do the washing up with Dotty, singing to David Bowie, talking about bands, boys and the places we dreamed of visiting. Maddy was very funny, and very honest.

Every night, I'd come home from the call centre and wonder what I was doing with my life. I'd scour the internet, looking for job adverts, and apply for every internship and junior writing job I could find. *You and Your Clay-Tiled Bathroom*, *Moth Fancier's Periodical* and *Junior Sudoku Challenge* all told me that I did not have enough experience to work for free. I was close to abandoning all hope, and resigning myself to a lifetime of being shouted at by angry people who believed their car insurance should be free, or that their seventeen-year-old children should be allowed to drive cars with four-litre engines, or that we should have all of the details of their policy even though they weren't with us and they really should be ringing Norwich Union. But then one evening, after a particularly depressing day at work, one job listing stood out. Sunlight streamed through the screen of the family computer. I could hear the 'Hallelujah Chorus'.

Bliss, the iconic teen girls' magazine, wanted a features intern – a *paid* features intern. At the time, I thought I might have more luck if I'd seen a job ad titled, 'Hey! Have you thought about winning the lottery?' But I *longed* for it. I fancied it. At the call centre, at the gym and in my sleep I dreamed about what my life would be like if I worked for *Bliss*. I knew that I wanted to write funny things for teenage girls more than anything. And I knew because I'd been hanging out with Maddy.

With great grace, Maddy embraced her role as the star of my focus group. She and Dotty gave me tutorials on My Chemical Romance, Miley Cyrus and the Jonas Brothers. When I opened my emails and discovered I had an interview, it was Maddy I hugged as I jumped for joy. When Leslie, the editor, asked me about the ultimate teenage crush of the moment, it was Maddy's bedroom walls I pictured when I answered 'Orlando Bloom'. When I got the job, and was eventually made a staff writer, Maddy interned for me for a week and came to stay in my flat. I remember bursting with tenderness and pride as we walked into the office together. (She looked incredibly cool and stylish in her flippy floral dress and white blazer; I looked slightly dishevelled in leggings, flip-flops and a free Lady Gaga T-shirt.) I remember bursting with irritation when we shared a pint of Ben and Jerry's to celebrate her first day, and she dropped chocolate ice cream on the carpet and then ground it in with her heel. But most of all, I was aware that our relationship had shifted. We were proper, grown-up friends hanging out together.

When I was a teenager, I would have committed many murders in order to spend a week working at a magazine, even if it was a mag about moths or Sudoku. Giving Maddy the chance to have a go was better yet. My job was the first toy I was truly excited to share, and Maddy was the very best person to give it to. Although she hasn't gone on to work in publishing, she used the work experience on her university application – she ended up doing English, like me. Now Maddy is doing a masters in arts curation and administration. It's taken her a little while to work out what feels comfortable, and how to know whether an ambition is real and worth pursuing. I can't tell her what to want, but I've got enough years on her to be able to tell her that it's normal to be confused about it. The little girl who seemed extremely certain of everything has become a young woman who realises it's OK to say, 'I don't know.' I could not be more proud of her.

Maddy facts

○ When Maddy is excited about eating something, which is often, she holds her hands in front of her chest, palms facing outwards, and waggles her fingers like Homer Simpson. Sometimes she simply says, 'Oooh, pasta! Homer fingers!'

○ Maddy has a comic knack for misremembering and combining phrases and proverbs. My personal favourites are: 'Let's not dance around the bush' and 'A little knowledge goes a long way'. Maddy's greatest ambition is to compete on *Catchphrase*.

○ If you don't include her hair, Maddy is about five feet six inches tall. If you do count her hair, she's six foot one.

○ If you want to summon Maddy, whether she's in the next room or fifty miles away, you can do so by playing 'Africa' by Toto. If she can hear it, she will come to you.

○ There are almost no photos of Maddy from her First Holy Communion because she spent the whole day furious and scowling, *even though* she and Dotty were the only sisters who were allowed to wear white tops and trousers, like tiny Bianca Jaggers, or miniature members of Steps. Maddy has no memory of what made her so grumpy. (Dotty spent the day beaming, because she spilled ice cream on her brand new top and was allowed to change into a shirt which bore a picture of a frog.)

CHAPTER FIFTEEN
Is It Bad to Be Bossy?

Only women are bossy. Men are assertive, exacting and sometimes controlling – and even though the last trait isn't a positive one, it implies that the controlling man is getting his way without being questioned. 'Bossy' isn't a straightforward descriptor, it's an accusation. And it comes with a suggestion of powerlessness. A bossy woman is obeyed resentfully, if she's obeyed at all. When you picture a bossy woman, you don't think of a captain of industry. You picture Violet Elizabeth Bott, stamping a patent leather shoe while her lip trembles in rhythm with the ruffles of her ankle sock.

The psychologist Adam Grant says, 'When young women get called bossy, it's often because they're trying to exercise power without status. It's not a problem that they're being dominant; the backlash arises because they're "overstepping" their perceived status.' As women, it's very difficult for us to raise our status because everything in the world seems designed to make us question our right to confidence and self-worth. When we go to the places where we would expect to find high-status women – boardrooms, governments and executive offices – we'll find an overwhelming number of high-status men, and the odd woman who has to deal with periodic accusations of bossiness. If the woman in question has any siblings, and she's ever tried to assert herself in their presence, she will have had a lifetime to get used to it.

For me, hearing the word 'bossy' is like feeling someone else's finger prodding a blackened bruise. When I was a child, it was constantly used as a way of negatively assessing my character. Sometimes, I heard it during tellings off, because of the way I'd behaved towards my little sisters. And sometimes it was used as quick character shorthand, a detail that defined me during introductions. 'Ah, Daisy, she's our eldest, so she's the bossy boots.' People would hear this and size me up, and I fancied that I could hear what they were thinking. Bossy girls were divas, prima donnas, stuck up, fussy, loud, demanding and overconfident. I inferred this quickly and instinctively, and I tried so very hard to be quiet, to think less of myself and to stop asking for things.

In 2014, the campaign group LeanIn introduced a movement called Ban Bossy. Launched by Sheryl Sandberg and the US Girl Scouts association, the campaign featured a series of organisations and high-profile women who pledged to never use the word, because it was thought to stigmatise girls and women, and deter and distract them from pursuing their ambitions. A video went viral which featured Beyoncé declaring, 'I'm not bossy. I'm the boss,' a slogan that Sinéad O'Connor was so taken with, she used it as the title of her 2014 album. Predictably, there was a backlash, with a group of other public figures and celebrities keen to reclaim the word bossy while redefining it and redirecting its power.

When I was born, in the mid-eighties, I think the Western world was at a weird point in terms of parenting. We were starting to slide into an incredibly child-centric mindset, with more than one agenda. Children were being given more opportunities than ever to experience joy, happiness and fun. However, the eighties was also an era of ramped-up capitalism. Everyone watched the film *Wall Street*, and seemingly stopped paying attention shortly after Gordon Gekko's line 'Greed is good', thinking that was the true message of the story. The writer and publisher Tina Brown talked about 'the go go eighties' (and I doubt that you can be the youngest ever editor of *Tatler*, the most celebrated woman in publishing and the person responsible for putting naked, pregnant Demi Moore on the cover of *Vanity Fair* without being accused of bossiness, even if not to your face).

It was a period in which bossiness and assertiveness were fashionable, and anyone who wasn't visibly pushing ahead was bound to get left behind. There was a tension in the air. How could you raise a girl to become successful and ambitious while making sure that she never did anything as vulgar as state her demands? I think my parents were so anxious that I would somehow be infected by the spirit of the age that they instilled a phobia of bossiness within me. I was made to feel as though it was slightly less terrible than murder, but a lot worse than shoplifting.

Even now, I feel a prickle of pride if a new acquaintance is surprised to learn that I'm the eldest, not the youngest sister, just because it makes me believe that I've managed to hide my awful, evil bossiness and shove it below the surface of my skin. If I concentrate really hard, I can pretend to be a girl who has never offended anyone with her demands, whose desires are easily met. Because that's what the cult of bossy is about. Making women feel ugly, ashamed and even unfeminine for daring to ask for more than the world is prepared to give them.

It is assumed that bossiness is the opposite of asking nicely. We're told there's a trick to negotiation, and that with the right combination of open questions, smiles and surprise statements we can somehow make people give us what they want before they realise we've asked for it. I think of Lorelei Lee in *Gentlemen Prefer Blondes* – even though the character is castigated for being a gold digger, the story suggests it is preferable for her to wheedle, flirt, cajole and manipulate in order to get her hands on a diamond tiara than to simply say 'that's what I want'. Lorelei's beauty and sneakiness seem much more effective than outright, ugly bossiness. Of course it's a satire, and a fable about the age it was written in, but I know I'm not the only little girl who watched it and believed every word – and vowed to be less bossy, more Lorelei. After all, everyone wants to be Marilyn and no one wants to be the old-fashioned poster girl for bossiness, Matron from the *Carry On* films.

However, I'm starting to realise that my fear of being bossy is holding me back. What's more, I owe it to my sisters to be bossy. Not in order to force them to play the games I want, and give me all of their chocolate buttons, but because I want them to see me taking charge of my life, and then go off and take charge of theirs. I'm so anxious about being perceived as bossy that I lose opportunities. I get paid less. Most importantly, I'm not contributing to a culture that is positive about women who pursue what they want and need.

Women have been waiting, and asking nicely, for thousands of years. It has not got us very far. Looking alluring in pink satin might temporarily attract the attention of the man of our dreams, but in the long run, it doesn't boost our bank balances – or, most importantly, lead us to freedom. Bossiness will. As a child, I thought bossiness was about demanding other people's toys, and your own way. Now I realise it's about demanding respect and attention. About shouting, instead of waiting and hoping to be heard. About remembering the study that showed men speak for 70 to 75 per cent of the time at meetings, and won't stop interrupting women. As a gender, bossiness is absolutely not our problem, but our anxiety around it has been stopping us from succeeding. Who came up with the idea that women who spoke up about their desires and beliefs were bossy? It certainly wasn't us!

I'm collecting bossy role models. There's Tina Fey, the writer, actor and *30 Rock* showrunner who wrote a memoir called *Bossypants*, which includes a story about her brilliantly bossy *SNL* colleague Amy Poehler. Fey writes that, in the writers' room, Poehler was trying out a joke that was 'dirty, loud and "unladylike"' and performer Jimmy Fallon told her to stop, that he didn't like it. Poehler's reply? 'I don't fucking care if you like it.' That, right there, is the bossy girl's credo. When we stop caring about who likes us, and what we do, we can be creatively free. Even as I write this, I feel the need to add panicky caveats. Please don't think I'm advocating that we all start being mean, or unprofessional, or begin shitting in the street! Here's the thing. If you've ever been frightened of accusations of bossiness, if you've ever consciously compromised, bitten your lip or eaten your way around a salad ingredient that you know you're allergic to, you can comfortably raise your bossiness game by several notches.

In 2014, Jill Abramson was fired from her position as executive editor of the *New York Times*. Rumours circulated that this was down to her 'bossiness' – which spookily coincided with other rumours that she had been making enquiries about why her pay and pension benefits were significantly less than that of her male predecessor. In a 2013 *Newsweek* profile, Abramson was described as being 'high-handed, impatient . . . and obstinate'. Firstly, I'd argue that those are the exact attributes that are necessary if someone is going to be effective and successful as an executive editor. Secondly, I doubt that she was any more high-handed, impatient and obstinate than the man she replaced. Abramson now covers politics for the *Guardian* and is a visiting lecturer at Harvard University. Being labelled 'bossy' by an unsympathetic public makes her another heroine, a pioneer for progress.

When I think of Abramson, I think of every features meeting I went to at *Bliss* magazine where every one of us would say, 'Sorry, these ideas are a bit shit, I didn't really spend enough time on them,' before producing ten pages of bold, witty, well-thought-out concepts. I think of the time I emailed the editor of a national magazine, saying it was unacceptable that I'd been paid four months late, before bursting into tears and worrying that I'd never be allowed to work for them, or anyone else, again. I think of the times my sisters have come home weeping, because they've been harassed by creeps on the bus, on the train or in the street, and been too scared to shout back. And I think about how it's so much easier, cheaper and nicer for everyone if we're not bossy, if we refuse to know our worth and shout out about it, and how women are tacitly encouraged to sacrifice themselves every single day so that men might become more comfortable, more powerful and more wealthy. When a woman like Abramson breaks through and embraces what is called bossiness, for success and survival, she is made an example of. It keeps the rest of us safely in cages that we're encouraged to construct ourselves.

Being bossy is scary. It doesn't go against my nature, exactly, but it goes against the part of my nature that I've been encouraged to suppress since I was born. I'm afraid that it might not work for me. If I were to start being 10 per cent bossier, would I be 50 per cent more successful, or just 100 per cent more disliked? The fear started when I began to be bossy to my sisters, so I've decided that I need to be bossy *for* them, instead.

If you're like me, and you're frightened to speak out on your own behalf, you could try speaking out for other women. The successful campaign to repeal the eighth amendment in the Republic of Ireland and allow women access to safe, legal abortion, is a brilliant example of bossiness. For hundreds of years, women in Ireland had been told that their right to health and bodily autonomy was less significant than the Church's right to make the rules. The women who spoke out about this were abused, humiliated and silenced, called names and accused of being insufficiently feminine. But they kept speaking out, *for their sisters.* They were bossy. They spoke up even though many people believed they didn't have sufficient status to do so. And even though thousands of people told them to play nice, shut up and go home, they kept telling people what they wanted, and refused to be ignored. They won.

All of my sisters have bossy streaks, and it makes me proud. It comes from a sense of what's right, and a belief in being kind. When Grace tells me how to cook something, I roll my eyes and occasionally fail to resist the impulse to tell her that I am three years older than her, and therefore three years more experienced in the ways of the Kenwood Chef. When Maddy tells me that I don't know how to make an Aperol Spritz, and that her method is superior and I need bigger ice cubes, I know that she's not trying to brag, but to save me from inferior cocktails and humiliation.

Whenever my sisters are bossy, it's because they're absolutely certain that they know better. That certainty is rare. We need to find one thing to be bossy about. It might be book recommendations, or scented candles, or the films of Will Ferrell. But we must hold on to that one tiny thing and be prepared to assert that we know our subject better than anyone else alive. Even if it's a combination of unearned confidence and nonsense. Because the harder we believe, the sooner we'll stop being called bossy, and we'll get a toehold on a rung of self-belief. The other thing we need to do is amplify each other. When President Obama was in office, the female staffers, who found themselves in the minority, made an effort to repeat each other's key points, while crediting their author. When you do this for another woman, you raise her status – so she stops being 'bossy' and becomes 'an authority'.

Ultimately, bossy girls and women are criticised and

humiliated by people who believe they're worth more, and they can't bear the idea that a woman might know more than they do – or know better. To tell someone off for being bossy is to infect them with self-doubt. If we can start questioning whether our bossy tendencies really are the problem that they have been packaged as, we can stop questioning every other part of our personalities. Now I know that being a bossy big sister is only bad if it stops your little sisters from being bossy too. Don't hide your bossiness under a bushel. And if you have a bossy sister, why not meet her game and raise it?

CHAPTER SIXTEEN

Are You Suffering from Big Sister Syndrome?

In 1998, my main hobby was going to the cinema and watching *Titanic*. In the latter part of the year, this was supplanted by a brand new hobby, which was watching *Titanic* on VHS. At the time of writing, it's twenty years since my *Titanic* days, and I still couldn't tell you whether I actually enjoyed the film or not. All I know is that I always cry uncontrollably when I hear the posh man lying to his children and telling them that there will be another boat for the daddies, and I've almost calmed down when I see the elderly couple in bed, holding hands as their room fills up with water, and I start all over again. Also, Kate Winslet as she was then would be one of my top three people to swap faces and bodies with, and when I got engaged, I was constitutionally incapable of referring to my intended in the traditional manner without channelling Kate yelling at Billy Zane, 'Don't speak to me that way! I'm your fee-yon-say!'

There was a two-week period in which I stopped watching *Titanic*, and that occurred when the impossibly soignée sixteen-year-old Céline came to stay, to promote our local twin town association, and to help my sisters and me with our terrible French. Céline, as I remember her, was about seven feet tall, and had the longest, blondest hair I'd ever seen outside *Eurotrash*. (My secret *Eurotrash* viewing would have been a proper hobby if it didn't depend so heavily on absent parents and the functioning of a staticky, terrestrial portable TV.) Céline let me have a little go on a cigarette and was very kind when I started dry heaving. She encouraged a tiny flirtation with a friend of hers called, improbably, Pierre – neither of us fancied each other, but we fancied the idea of being fancied – and ended things speedily and stylishly when Pierre was spotted pointing at my chest and miming the act of testing the ripeness of avocados in a supermarket.

Spending time with Céline was a bit like being briefly fostered by a big sister. I can't remember if she had des frères ou des soeurs (although I'm pretty sure she had trois animaux à la maison, un chien et deux chats). But I'd be surprised if she didn't have younger siblings, because she instinctively saw me and took care of me, in a kindly, slightly bossy way. I loved it. I didn't even mind being bossed about, because, as someone who was three years my senior, she had earned that right. I'd have given her power of attorney, simply because she was born in 1982.

Back on RMS *Titanic*, my own bossiness was being called into question. One of the reasons for the constant watching was that it was constantly on, everywhere anyone went, in 1998. You'd go to see your cousins, and they might give you a vague wave from the floor of the sitting room, their hands cupping their chins, before shouting, 'QUIET! He's about to draw her naked, in the nude!' and you'd stop, drop and roll as silently as possible in order to join them on the floor without drowning out the sound of Leo's pencil strokes. You'd see an auntie or uncle who didn't have children and were quite anxious to prove their cool credentials among sulky teens. They'd coo, 'I've got a surprise for you! Have you seen this film, *Titanic*? It's very popular!' Then, every single time you saw your friends outside school, at each sleepover, or whenever you slumped, unappealingly, on their parents' sofas, sticky from unsuccessfully trying on the entire stock of the Dolphin Centre branch of Mark One, someone would put it on. *Titanic*'s box office gross was $2.5 billion, and honestly, that number doesn't seem high enough. Half of that came from the efforts of the residents of Poole and Bournemouth.

During one of these post-shopping trip *Titanic* viewings, a fight broke out. Abby (who played lacrosse at county level and was doomed to spend her early teens constantly cast as the group Sporty Spice) picked up a bowl of Butterkist and screamed, 'SHUT UP! WILL YOU TWO SHUT UP? If you don't stop doing that I'm going to chuck this AT YOUR HEAD!'

She was shouting at me and our friend Olivia (the world's most improbable Ginger Spice, a bookish strawberry blonde who loved chemistry, sailing and Alistair MacLean novels).

'What? What are we doing?' asked Olivia, dazed.

'You're reading the film out! Every time, you read the film out! I know when it's present day! I can see the menus in the dining hall too! I don't care which coach company made the coach that they're bonking in!'

After a few minutes, Olivia and I realised that we'd been annoying everyone with a symptom of Big Sister Syndrome. We'd grown up watching films with little sisters, who were at varying stages of learning to read, and we'd drifted into the habit of helpfully doing their reading for them. This is kind of OK if your viewing companion is three, and your chosen entertainment is *Pingu*. Otherwise, it makes people murderous. Olivia and I would have been lucky to take a bowl of popcorn to the head.

If you've ever experienced Big Sister Syndrome, you're probably an infuriatingly excellent bullshitter. A little knowledge is a dangerous thing, and when you have the right answer 40 per cent of the time, simply because you're slightly more mature and experienced than the person asking, it's very tempting to make up the rest, and invent convenient truths for them because you're drunk on power. Big Sister Syndrome is also infused with bossy benevolence. You're constantly answering questions that nobody asked because you genuinely want to help. I think you're less likely to suffer from it if you have a single sibling. When you're focusing your bossy energies on a single person, they're much more likely to snap, retaliate and challenge you so that every fact you foist upon them becomes a debate. However, if you're the first reference point for several small people, your completely pretend, nonsense authority is endorsed. You create a system of Russian dolls for fake news, each one backed with a purer, more distilled quantity of bollocks, as your well-meaning lie is passed down from sister to sister.

I've worked in offices where I've seen Big Sister Syndrome at play. It just takes one self-assured, self-appointed grown-up to create a cult in which ten or more adult women start drinking vinegar in the morning, or painting their nails beige, or develop a communal crush on a cartoon horse. My mum (who is, after all, the mother of big sisters, having given birth to five of them – an even fiercer label than 'mother of dragons') once had the big sister treatment from a friend of a friend after dinner. Mum's request for a post-prandial espresso caused confusion and consternation among the waiting staff, so the would-be big sister patted Mum's hand and said, 'She means a cappuccino.' Poor Mum had to suffer the indignity of being publicly condescended to, *and* she had to digest a big mug of frothy milk after 11 p.m.

Because I'm a big hypocrite, I bristle a bit when I'm being Big Sistered myself. Surely no one is a bigger big sister than me. I have true credentials! Five of them! However, there's something deeply comforting about being told what to do. Right now, I wish I had a big sister who could peer over my shoulder and say, 'What are you doing? Write this!'

Sometimes, I fantasise about having the perfect big sister. She'd be a bit like me, just older. She'd buy me expensive, fabulously thoughtful gifts, she'd lend me money and never expect me to pay it back, and she'd take me out for big, boozy lunches and tell me that she *knows* everything is going to work out brilliantly for me, that she knew just the person who would shoot my career trajectory skyward, and did I want their email address? The closest I ever got to finding this mythical big sister was when I proudly tweeted about having an almost full complement of wooden clothes hangers, and I got an avalanche of unsolicited advice from women telling me to switch to velvet. (Unsolicited advice is the most heavily devalued currency of the twenty-first century. It's worth nothing, we can get it by the wheelbarrow, but we shall never go short of it.)

My perfect big sister model has changed the way I behave

as a sibling. It's a privilege to be in a position where I can give my sisters some of the things I wish someone would give me. To be able take them to Topshop and say, 'All this, my son, I mean sister, could be yours! Well, you can pick one thing but stay away from the Unique section and the leather jackets.' To listen to their break-up stories, and hold them in my arms until we're both saturated with snot, and be able to say, 'I *know* you don't believe me but I can promise, on both our lives, that you feel horrible now because you're definitely going to feel OK soon, that this is not the end of your story.' To say: 'The world will not end if you quit your horrible job – in fact, things will *begin*! You're too bright and beautiful and talented for work to make you this unhappy, I'll help you make a plan, I can lend you some rent money.'

Almost every day, I live with acute anxiety, the certainty that there are bad times just around the corner, and I would do *anything* to prevent my sisters from experiencing this pain in their lives, even if it means that I am essentially an unqualified therapist and unlimited overdraft facility.

This is a well-intentioned act of love, but it's not necessarily a happy, healthy one. Unusually, I don't feel as though any of my sisters have ever taken advantage of this, but I know of plenty of families where siblings do exploit each other. My friend Tara tells me, 'I'm ten years older than my little sister. She's at the beginning of her career, she's really ambitious and wants to work in film. I live in south London, and I have my own small, two-bedroom flat. My sister Megan doesn't have her own place, and she officially lives with Mum and Dad in Leicester, but she stays with me constantly, while she's being a runner, or an intern. At first, I was absolutely delighted to be in a position to give her a bit of a leg up, but it's been awful. Although she had housemates at uni, she's not really used to living with anyone as an adult. She's not deliberately awful, but she's not considerate; she has to be asked to clean up and she expects me to drop everything and put her up when an opportunity comes her way. I asked Mum and Dad to have a word, but they told me off for "squabbling" – I'm thirty-five! I don't think I could ever turn Megan down; she's my baby sister. But it's difficult to work out a way of saving our relationship. If she was just a 25-year-old housemate who was paying me rent, I think the dynamic would be totally different.'

The biggest problem with Big Sister Syndrome is that those of us who experience it have a tendency to take responsibility for other people's wellbeing, and feelings. As an agony aunt, I'd tell Tara to talk to her sister. As a big sister myself, I understand how very difficult that would be. We have a tendency to act *in loco parentis*, and we want to be the Cool Moms we never had – and when we share parents we know exactly which gaps we want to fill in, and where our own mothers are lacking in coolness.

Like Tara, I have a problem with establishing boundaries. My own sisters have never overstepped the mark, but sometimes I've struggled to maintain friendships with younger women because my urge to be a big sister takes over. I don't think it's better to give than to receive, but it's certainly easier, and I've engineered a difficult dynamic into every one of these relationships because while I know how to provide unconditional love and lunch, I don't know how to ask for these things.

Taking is tricky. When someone offers something to me, I panic, and try to outdo them in order to keep the balance in my favour. If someone invites me to dinner, I will bring two bottles of wine, a bottle of champagne, flowers, hummus, olives and a family-sized trifle, partly because the debt of gratitude causes me physical pain, and partly because if they're my actual little sister I'm not confident that they will have remembered to switch the oven on.

However, I think that while being a sister has exacerbated that problem for me, it's a problem that women face all over the world. We're conditioned to be givers. We're the absorbent, emollient task force that has been made to feel as though life as we know it would end if we were to display any behaviour that seemed greedy, thoughtless or selfish. I feel obliged to help every woman I meet who seems to need it, whether or not she asks, because I believe it's a feminist act. However, learning how to take would also be a feminist act.

Perhaps many of us slip into Big Sister Syndrome because we long to feel needed. It's a power issue, too. Even when you're giving everything you have to help someone else, you can feel bolstered by the act of being the giver and the doer, as well as telling yourself that you're strong by comparison. You're less vulnerable than the person you're helping. Giving helps us to maintain an illusion of control, an experience that it can be hard for women to harness in other ways. But maybe, if anyone has the answers, it's our little sisters.

My younger sisters have two magnificent life skills, and I'm trying hard to master them both. They are better than me at asking questions, and at saying, 'No, I can't do that.' It's all about setting boundaries, which can be a life-saving act.

Are You Suffering from Big Sister Syndrome?

When we don't have boundaries, and when we define ourselves by the idea that we'll do anything for anyone, our own outlines start to dissolve. For a long time, our culture has celebrated the women who do this, and castigated the women who rebel against the idea. Big Sister Syndrome is very convenient for the patriarchy, because it makes it easy to walk all over women while letting them believe they're in control.

There have been times when I wished I could be my own big sister, an idea that was crystallised when I was eight, and discovered Hunter Davies' *Flossie Teacake* series on the school bookshelf. The eponymous nine-year-old heroine *longs* to be like her wild, glamorous eighteen-year-old sister Bella – and discovers what Bella's life is like when a magical fur coat makes Flossie eighteen too. Of course, Flossie soon learns that being eighteen is equal parts stupendous, glittery fun and devastating, awkward hell. I was a great fan of Flossie's ingenuity – for example, she claims that her teachers have introduced a new shoe into the school dress code, the 'Style Etto', and Flossie is wobbling around the shoe shop in five-inch heels before her mum realises she's been had. Bella is mean to Flossie, and keeps her sister away from her world, and so Flossie's eighteen-year-old alter ego becomes an auxiliary sibling, providing Flossie with the information and experience she longs for.

Who would you become, for a few hours, if you slipped on a stolen fur coat? What would you like to find out about yourself? Even if you *have* a big sister, you can imagine Future You, the person who knows you better than anyone, the advice that they would give you and the stories that they would have to tell.

My Secret Big Sister self is, I imagine, a woman who gives far fewer fucks than me. She doesn't want me to be a doormat. She wants me to be kind, always, but to learn a way of being kind that doesn't come at the cost of self-preservation. She wants me to preserve my outlines in platinum and titanium, and to be much more careful about how I bend to accommodate others. Ultimately, she knows how fierce I am about protecting my little sisters and she wants me to be just as ferocious when it comes to protecting myself. Flossie's big sister Bella is a bad big sister, and a brilliant one. Leading by example, she teaches Flossie to be independent, slightly brutal, and to stop giving everything away. Bella wouldn't give Flossie the coat off her back, and so, in order to understand her own story, Flossie has to take it.

The characteristics we associate with being a big sister – generosity, bossiness and the desire to make everything perfect for everyone – are personality traits that most of us have traces of. Sometimes they're brilliant, and they boost us and make us forces for good in the lives of many people. But they can hold us back and prevent us from pushing for what we want because they lead us to invest all of our energy in other people. If you feel like a big sister, it means that you're defined by the people you're hoping to help. We need to work out a way of helping ourselves too. We can learn to be generous with ourselves, and provide ourselves with the nourishment and support that we feel obliged to provide other people with. We can be bossy with ourselves, and make sure we get our jobs done. We can't make anything perfect for anyone, but we can make life a lot better for ourselves if we stop taking so much responsibility for the lives of others.

Dotty

Sometimes I think that being a twin must be like being a sister on steroids. Every atom of anxiety about sharing, jealousy, judgement and the assumption of others gets revved up and multiplied. People become fixated on and fascinated with difference. 'You're so unlike the other one! You are up and she is down, you are here and she is there, *how can this be?*' Wouldn't it be weirder if you stayed symbiotic, if you didn't pull apart, if you didn't, at times, define yourself by your opposition to your other?

So it is that Dotty has spent too much of her life being defined as Not Maddy. For a long time, the two girls shared their friends, hobbies and obsessions, and suffered the indignity of parents evenings in which teachers, who should have known better, talked to my parents about the fact that they aren't identical in looks, regardless of their talents and temperaments.

All of my sisters are very beautiful, but I think Dotty's beauty sneaks up on people because she doesn't announce it herself. For a long time, I mistook Dotty's demeanour for shyness. However, I think that she's learned that when you're the last in a long line of mouthy women, you can learn a lot by holding back and speaking selectively. Because of this, many men fancy Dotty in a way that makes me want to grind their bones to dust. I've seen them talking to her as though they're writing a TripAdvisor review, and she's the gem of a secret bar on the beach that only they know about, because all of the other lads are necking watery Super Bock in Las Ramblas. Dotty has absolutely no time for this nonsense. Once, we were having drinks when a friend of a friend, a fairly well-known media personality who should have known better (and had a good thirty years on Dotty) started making significant overtures towards her. If I were in her position at that point in my twenties, I would have had my head turned, simply by my proximity to his power. Dotty simply rolled her eyes and whispered, 'Let's go to the bar, away from this *really annoying man*.'

Dotty met her Big Love, Mike, when she was really young. It was the start of the summer holidays, a couple of months after her fourteenth birthday, and Mike, who had met Dotty through friends, had invited her to go to Nando's. There was some familial handwringing, partly because fourteen is quite young for any kind of dating, and partly because Dotty was and is the baby of the bunch. Once the littlest is eating Macho Peas with a Macho Man, you've reached a point where the whole clan should be joining hands and singing, 'I'm Not a Girl, Not Yet a Woman.'

Significantly, I think, Maddy didn't have a date, and didn't *seem* to mind, even though I wanted to mind on her behalf. After all, I knew exactly why I got a boyfriend when I was fifteen – it was so I could have a part of my life that seemed like *mine,* and I couldn't be expected to share it with my sisters. My first boyfriend was nerdy, intense and prone to lengthy, mysterious sulks, but he wanted to go out with me, and that was enough. However, I think Dotty saw my mistakes and made better choices. Mike is calm, considerate and balanced. They have plenty of shared interests that go beyond 'each other'. Their relationship is still going strong.

Sometimes I wonder whether Dotty was initially quick to embrace the label of 'girlfriend' because it was a refreshing change from 'littlest sister, youngest twin'. It marked a chapter of quiet rebellion, which ended, I think, when Dotty decided not to go to university. I worried about her, in a way that was quite invasive. I didn't understand why my clever sister didn't want to dash out into the world as quickly as she could. In my head, I had intense, furious conversations with Mike, in which I accused him of holding her back. Dotty simply didn't know what she wanted to do, so she waited until she did, and went to study film at Brighton.

She's much, much wiser than I am. I wish I could be more like her, better at tuning out the 'shoulds' and 'oughts', able to trust myself to stop every so often, instead of constantly hurrying forwards in a panic, because I'm frightened that I'll lose all momentum forever. Dotty doesn't make bad choices, because she allows herself to be thoughtful, and she understands that finding the best answers is different from finding the fastest ones. It's a rare quality, and one that is becoming increasingly precious. Dotty is a film editor, and her ability to make strong, long-lasting decisions is reflected in the quality of her work. Again, it took a little while for her to work out what she wanted to do, but when she chose, she chose extremely well. She's found a career that's stimulating, satisfying and uses her talents fully. Through Dotty, I've learned that holding back and taking your time to think things through might make you bad at musical chairs, but it makes you very good at everything else in life.

At points, I think the whole family have been guilty of underestimating Dotty, defining her by her place at the end of the line, and not by her brain. However, instead of bemoaning this, Dotty plays it to her advantage, having developed a sense of humour that's somewhere on a scale between subversive and evil. When she and Maddy were at school, a streaker ran through the playground, which generated a solid month's worth of gossip as it happened when national paedophile paranoia was at its height. (Almost adorably, the twins and their friends confused their words and kept referring to the suspected paedophile as a 'poltergeist'.) Maddy was in the kitchen after school, telling Mum: 'The poltergeist had a sock over his willy, it was one of those big slipper socks, and he went into Mr Choolop's office, and he took the sock off, and threw it in his face!'

Dotty strolled in, opened the fridge, poured herself a glass of orange juice and laughed. 'No he didn't! Maddy, I started that rumour!'

That's sisterhood. You need someone to make up the story, and someone else to spread it and believe it.

Dotty facts

- Dotty loves and adores bears. She likes bears more than most people. At any given moment, if you ask her what she's thinking, it will be about bears. She's watched the harrowing Werner Herzog documentary *Grizzly Man* at least five times, and she believes that 'dying peacefully of old age, in your sleep' is an inferior way to die when compared with 'being killled and eaten by grizzly bears'. However, she holds polar bears in mysterious contempt.

- Occasionally I will look at our family WhatsApp and realise I haven't had a proper word-based chat with Dotty for weeks. We will have communicated entirely in *Peep Show* and *Simpsons* gifs.

- Dotty's favourite ever *Drag Race* contestant is Alaska Thunderfuck, and her second favourite is Sharon Needles.

- I would estimate that 40 per cent of Dotty's wardrobe is made from waterproof neoprene. She is not a scuba diver.

- Dotty rarely asks me for advice, but she sometimes asks me about the welfare of the baby iguanas on *Blue Planet*. I will always protect her delicate eyes and ears from racer snakes.

CHAPTER SEVENTEEN
Sisters in Love and Law

'I wasn't expecting you to kiss me then,'
I said, many months later.

'I wasn't expecting to kiss you either,' he replied.
'But I thought you were worth being brave for.'

When you have five sisters, it means that when you fall in love with someone, they have to consider the possibility of acquiring five sisters too. Five versions of you who might be prettier, or funnier, or more extreme and off-putting versions of the most irritating version of you. Your sisters will not necessarily conspire to cast the most flattering glow on your personality, and you might well explode with the effort of negotiating your two separate selves. The adult, attractive boyfriend haver, and the inarticulate delinquent given to ineffectual acts of violence. Also, your sisters will see this effort, and find it humiliating (Beth), alienating (Grace), boastful (Liv), cringe-inducing (Maddy), or simply baffling (Dotty) on your behalf. After seeing my efforts to integrate my first boyfriend with the family, Beth vowed that she would never, ever allow a romantic partner to meet any of us. Her words were: 'You won't know who I am going out with unless I die, and then you might see him at the funeral, even though I will leave him strict instructions not to talk to you. It will be my dying wish.'

I shall call my first boyfriend William, after Mr Collins in *Pride and Prejudice*. Like Mr Collins, my William could talk for hours on end, without worrying about whether he was being boring, or whether anyone actually wanted to listen to him. Also like Mr Collins, I suspect that William would have gone out with any one of us, and I just happened to be the sister he was introduced to first.

As a teenager, there had been three things that I wanted most in the world. A boyfriend, a job and a mobile phone. When I met William shortly after my fifteenth birthday, I assumed that this was the result of some Noel Edmonds-style cosmic ordering, and the job and the phone would soon follow. (They did, not because the universe had granted me any favours, but because, in the case of the former, the scope of my ambition was quite small, and with the latter, I won some money with an anecdote that was published in the 'Studied Wit' section of the *Reader's Digest*, and spent it all on a Nokia 3210.) I assumed Beth would be cripplingly jealous of my adult status. It took me a long time to realise she had a lot more self-respect than I did. She was holding out for a boyfriend she liked. I would have gone out with a Prince Charles mask Blu-Tacked to a broom handle if I thought there was a chance that someone might have seen me from a distance and thought, 'Ah, look at that girl with a boyfriend! She seems popular and normal!'

For a time, my relationship with William made me feel

very separate from my sisters. I chose him, or rather, he chose me, and my sisters could never make me feel chosen. We simply had to tolerate each other, and I didn't make an effort to make them feel adored, or even endured. I just invested all of my emotional energy in my first teenage relationship. Later, Grace told me, 'I didn't like it, and although I wouldn't have put it this way at the time, I did feel as though William was taking you away from us – and you wanted to be taken away. Even when you were here with us, you wouldn't be funny or silly any more. I had crushes, and boys I liked, but at the back of my mind I worried that it would happen to me if I got a boyfriend, so I didn't want one.'

Eventually I broke up with William. It took six years, seven jobs and three phones. We'd followed each other to university, miserably, but reminding each other that we couldn't possibly break up with each other, because it would be 'a waste'. It's thanks to William that I truly understand the meaning of the expression 'to throw good money after bad'. We threw good time after bad. Looking back, it made as much sense as saying: 'But the house fire has been going for three hours now, it seems a shame to put it out after all that time!'

William could be incredibly cruel. Worse still, he was annoying. More annoying than every single one of my sisters on a hot five-hour car journey multiplied by a school shoe-shopping trip. I was cruel and annoying too – after all, when we met, he was a teenage boy and I was a teenage girl. The problems were obvious. Still, after I said that I had to end it, for a fairly shallow reason – I was sick of coming home after lectures and seeing him in a dressing gown, playing *Zelda* with the curtains drawn – I braced myself for the drop. I had loved him with all my heart, and I'd given something away by mistake. I would always be a little bit broken. I could never love again. I spent a five-hour cross-country train journey gazing moodily out the window, listening to Dusty Springfield singing 'Ne Me Quitte Pas'. I wasn't quite sad enough not to admire my reflection – I felt *beautifully* tragic, in a way that had nothing to do with my face and everything to do with the glossy, cinematic, forgiving quality of a Virgin Voyager window.

'Are you OK?' asked Beth, also home for university holidays, before giving me an unusually long, Herbal Essences-scented hug. Grace brought me a cup of tea. Liv offered me a cigarette, which I declined. 'You know what, I'm a bit sad, but I mostly feel relieved. I think it's going to be all right.'

'Good!' said Beth. 'Because if you miss him *I can talk about Pink Floyd in a really annoying voice*, and if you try to escape and go to the loo, *I can continue talking through the door.*' Beth's impression of William was really mean, and really good. Imagine Eeyore, but pompous.

Grace added, 'I've been working on some anime-inspired art, cartoons and things. Beth, why don't you tell me everything I've got wrong, *but really slowly.*'

Liv looked thoughtful. 'I know! And I can sneak pervy looks at everyone's boobs.'

Within an hour, I was fine.

After William, my one true love, the man who meant there could be no other for me, there was Dave. Dave was an Ultimate Frisbee player who dumped me for his housemate

Betty, who became one of my best friends. Then there was Mark, the sweet but boring banker who was fully freaked out by my charming, noisy, demanding family. Then, oh, let's call him Voldemort, the boy that didn't break my heart, but pulverised it over and over, who put me down and dismissed me and made me doubt myself so strongly that on some days, I couldn't have told you my name.

It was when I was trying and failing to recover, and I couldn't work out how to put myself back together, or stop making bad decisions, that Grace told me she was getting married. She accidentally gave me the greatest relationship advice I have ever heard. 'I know you probably think I'm too young, but I think I'm doing the right thing – Ed is the kindest person I have ever met.' For the first time, I realised where I'd been going wrong. I'd been lying to myself about who I was, and what I wanted. Grace had always been sure. It was time to admit that the most grown-up thing I could do was ask for help from my baby sister.

I thought about my boyfriends, and my sisters' boyfriends. We all treated each other's partners with suspicion. Beth was having a mysterious affair with a man who lived in Prague. She told us very little about him. He lived with his mum, they had an outdoor toilet, and when she saw him she ate a lot of butter, because it was the most luxurious and rare commodity in his world and he wanted her to have something precious. She didn't have the heart or Czech vocabulary to explain that it wasn't usually eaten with a spoon.

Liv had terrible luck, and went out with a succession of boys who seemed to treat her appallingly, one being an amateur bigamist who worked as a mechanic. (When he failed to turn up to her birthday party, a panic-stricken Liv imagined him under the wheels of a car, or lost at sea. She rang him thirty times, and his other girlfriend picked up on the thirty-first.) Maddy's last truly horrible boyfriend had sustained a minor injury after he stopped to admire himself in the wing mirror of a car without noticing that its driver had returned and was reversing out of their parking space.

Grace and Dotty both seemed to have stumbled upon a brilliant secret to happiness. Don't go out with someone unless they are *kind to you*. It doesn't matter if they're the hottest person that you've ever seen in your life, or even the funniest. Kindness must be at their core. Everything else is icing. Sure, they might be nice to you at the very beginning because they fancy you, but there are clues in how they treat other people, and it's worth paying attention, because this is how they will treat you when you stop being new and thrilling. Mark the banker did not tip waiting staff. Voldemort openly flirted with other women, shouted at his mother and refused to RSVP anything on principle, in case a better invitation came his way. Maddy's bad boyfriend thought that Wayne Rooney was 'a legend' and Liv's would call her from his car to make her come outside, instead of meeting her family. (He also refused to tell her his real last name.)

I think that many young women get lost in our twenties. We start in the middle of a metaphorical sea, and we allow ourselves to follow a bad navigational path, led by someone who is just as lost as we are, but who has been told a different story and made to hide their vulnerability entirely instead of letting themselves be suffocated by it. This is just as damaging. We believe we're lucky to be loved, even loved badly, and we'll follow cruel masters to the end of the earth because we don't know that it's OK to stop, take stock and stay by ourselves for a while. We let ourselves be led by people who need to be followed, those who are lost too, but think that our love might save them from their own self-hatred. We're all trying to escape ourselves, and compensate for our own inability to be kind to ourselves. If we were able to stop for a second, and remember to choose carefully instead of simply feeling lucky to be chosen, we wouldn't end up miles from the shoreline, feeling hopeless and beyond rescue.

Perhaps some of my sisters, like me, chose badly because we knew so little about love. As the eldest, I thought I was the wisest. I was crushed by my failure to care for myself, and to protect the others from my mistakes. It was Grace who was quiet enough and strong enough to know, instinctively, to wait for real love, and to appreciate the still water instead of rushing towards the bigger splash.

Six months after Grace got engaged, I met a kind man. He made plans with me and kept them, he brought me thoughtful gifts, he called often and listened when I talked. One night, he took me to the theatre. I had a mild spring cold which mutated into something fluey over the course of the interval. He took me all the way home to Streatham, kissed me gently outside my flat, and went home, all the way to Walthamstow.

Grace was excited for me. 'How's it going? Do you like him?'

I frowned. 'I do, but . . . he's a bit keen.'

Grace paused. I could hear her, rolling her eyes. 'What do you mean, "keen"?'

'You know, he's just . . . really nice to me. Too nice. I mentioned a book I wanted to read, in passing, and he bought it for me! Isn't that creepy?'

'Are you saying that he's kind to you?'

Kindness is an unsung virtue. It's easy to devalue. It's not something we give awards for, we don't put it on our CVs, and we're slow to praise it in other people. In fact, when people are kind, we often accuse them of having some sort of agenda. The concept of kindness makes us cynical. We think it's an act of manipulation, that it's the opposite of honesty. Perhaps that's why so many of us don't know how to be kind to ourselves. We worry that doing so would be delusional, and believe it's better to be cruel and uncompromisingly honest, than it is to see the best in ourselves and in others.

This idea is holding humanity back. And it means that we're making love very difficult for ourselves.

Because of Grace, I married the kind man on a crisp autumn day. I've never stopped being grateful for my brilliant luck – in finding him, and in having the sort of sister who is much more compassionate and clear-sighted than I am.

Not long after the conversation with Grace, he met the family, almost by accident. The plan was that he would pick me up in the pub after Grace's hen party, and we'd go out for dinner, and go dancing. The plan went wrong, and when Dale arrived at the pub, my mum was still there. So was her sister, my auntie, a handful of cousins and most of my sisters – including Beth, who had skipped the afternoon tea in order to protest the aesthetic dominance of the macaron, or something. I didn't think she was coming to the party at all. She had been to see her boyfriend, in Prague, and got a Megabus to London, to 'surprise' Grace. It took three days. Beth was perversely proud of the fact that her boyfriend didn't have any plumbing in his flat. She was also wearing her favourite charity shop find, a full-length waxed Barbour that was designed to repel all human contact. Beth *stank*. It was a multi-layered, complex, challenging bouquet of wet dog, forgotten tuna sandwich, manure and bin day. She smelled like an armpit's armpit.

At the time, I'd been dating Dale for a little under two months. It had been going really well, but I was still nervous enough about our nascent relationship to really care about things like stinky sisters. Accidentally ambushing him with half of my family was not ideal, but it would be OK if he found them charming, a delightful extension of Lovely Me. There was every chance that he would be put off, perhaps forever, if he met a version of me that couldn't be tolerated unless he was prepared to breathe through his mouth for an extended period.

The situation might have been more bearable if Beth had done what I would do in her position – acknowledge it, and make up a funny, faintly plausible lie. You know: 'I'm so sorry that I smell like something that died in a drainpipe, I accidentally stepped in a manhole and fell into some sewage on the way over. I had to walk underground, through poo, all the way from Chelsea. Let me tell you, that poo does *not* smell as posh as you might think!' Also, I was in a very bad mood with Beth, who had been a real dick about Grace's hen party, and acted as though the activity had been chosen to spite her. 'I'm not the kind of girl who eats cupcakes for fun,' she hissed, which made me imagine her eating a bun with grey icing, wrapped in barbed wire, chewing with her mouth open and saying, 'See, cake should make you miserable!' Beth seemed to believe that organising a party for Grace had been a lovely holiday for me, and I'd spent the last three months throwing shiny pink streamers up in the air and singing 'I enjoy being a girl!' instead of emailing twenty-three people I barely knew and saying, 'So sorry to bother you again but you said you'd send over the £27.33 last Thursday, and if we don't have it by tomorrow we can't go.'

Other new boyfriends would have met Beth, got a whiff of the Barbour and suddenly remembered that they had agreed to go and work in Zurich for the next eighteen months. Beth also got very, very drunk, very quickly. I sat and seethed as she demanded that Dale go and get her another pint, when she had not bought a single round. I danced around her, ineffectually spraying Dior Forever and Ever in a metre radius around her, but I could not beat the Barbour. At one point Dale asked Beth where she was staying while she was in London. 'Oh, I'll stay at Daisy's,' she replied. 'In fact, I'm ready to go now.' It is only fair to point out that when Beth lived in Zone 2, before I moved to London, I was constantly taking advantage of her good nature and sofa. It wasn't just mean of me to resent my unexpected hosting duties, it was downright hypocritical. Still, not only was she derailing my night by inviting herself to stay, but my flat was so small, sad and grotty that we didn't even have a sofa. She'd have to share my bed, and I'd have to Febreeze her before she got in.

I opened my mouth. I closed it again. I counted to ten,
then to twenty, then made a prolonged hissing sound. Then I
wailed, 'But we had PLANS!' Dale smiled bravely. 'That's
OK, we can do it another time. I'll head back too. Beth, it
was really lovely to meet you, I hope I see you again soon.'
He hugged her, unreservedly. And then he hugged me
tenderly. 'I'll call you tomorrow,' he said, and I knew he
meant it. He'd seen the worst version of me – not in Beth,
but in the person I became around Beth, the shallow,
neurotic, insecure person who was sometimes very bad at
loving the people I was supposed to love. And he wasn't going
anywhere.

Beth came back home with me, and we had the biggest
fight of our lives – even though we weren't actually biting
each other, we were as bitchy and as bitter as we could be. I
told her I was embarrassed by her and ashamed of her, and
she told me that if Dale was a good man it wouldn't affect
the way he felt about me, and if I thought it did, I was
wasting my time. She was right. The next morning, we made
it up very, very slowly, over pancakes. I longed for a Lifetime
Movie conclusion of sisterly contrition, but we called a thin-
lipped truce: Beth would stop going on about how boringly
conventional, profligate and girly I was if I stopped visibly
wrinkling my nose when I was downwind of her.

After dropping Beth off at Brixton tube station, I met
Dale at the cinema. I didn't know what to say, and whether I
should apologise for my sister. Clumsily, I started with, 'About
last night . . .'

Dale cut me off and said, smiling, 'I really liked her!' He
added 'It reminded me of when I was on tour with a band

and we drove across the West Coast with a hole in the bottom of the car, and we all started hallucinating from petrol fumes.' That night, after a harrowing Aki Kaurismäki comedy and three big glasses of wine, I told Dale I loved him, and he told me he loved me too. Then the next morning, while we were drinking coffee, he said, 'I want to say it again, soberly, because I really mean it. I do love you.'

Suddenly it was summer, then it was December, and Dale had fully bonded with every single sister. He found a point of connection with each of them, in a way that no boyfriend had bothered to do before, behaving like the platonic ideal of a big brother. He laughed at jokes, he bought rounds, he asked thoughtful questions and was unstintingly, tirelessly kind. He spent Christmas with my family, the very first time I'd had a boyfriend home for the holidays. I wasn't the only one.

On Boxing Day, Beth had a guest. A broad-shouldered, softly spoken, smiley guest who liked corduroy trousers, real ale and military history. But it was clear that he loved Beth a million times more than all of these things combined. Beth, who seemed so keen to convince us all that she was spiky, unconventional and horrified by anything sentimental, had fallen hard. After years of secretive, unsuccessful flings with nihilist punk poets, squat dwellers and men who wanted to woo her with dairy products, she was in love with a man that she wanted us all to meet. A man who not only drove, but had a car, and car insurance. A man who looked like he'd probably buy new toothpaste and toilet roll before he'd run out of his existing supply. We all loved him too – because he was nice and kind, and because he loved her fiercely and without condition. To everyone's delight, and Dad's bank manager's consternation, Dale and I were married in the autumn, and Beth and James were married in the following spring.

Perhaps oddly, neither Dale nor my two new brothers-in-law have any biological sisters. I suspect this is a complete coincidence, but I wonder whether it made it easier for them to inherit a full set of five new female sort-of-siblings. I love my new brothers, not just because they make my sisters so happy, but because they help me to see my sisters in a new light. They have built homes with their husbands, filled with love and yet entirely different, with no link between them apart from the pictures on the bookshelf. Beth's house is full of vintage quilts, seventies crockery and naval memorabilia. Grace's is a palace of gadgets, grown-up Lego and fantasy books. They have found love with people who reflect their true selves back to them, who understand them in ways that I will never be able to. This should make me desperately sad, but it makes sense, and it makes me love them as women and friends, as well as sisters.

When Dale sees me with my sisters, he sees me at my best and my worst. He's watched me swollen with love, incandescent with irrational rage, and completely insensible with laughter. He knows I will give my last tenner in the world to my sisters, but I will draw their blood in order to get to the last custard cream. I hope that they see me differently too, now that I love and am loved by the best person I've ever known. That love has made me softer, stronger, and more confident in my own vulnerability.

As a teenager, I wished that my sisters were jealous of my

love life. After all, what was the point of having a boyfriend unless they wanted one too? (They didn't, and they certainly didn't want a William.) As a wife, I don't want my girls to envy me. In the past, I've envied them their romantic happiness, but love dissolves jealousy as quickly as sherbet dissolves on your tongue. I don't think they necessarily need to have partners to be happy, but I do want them to love themselves fiercely enough to choose their Big Loves wisely. Love should make you bolder and louder. Too many women are offered conditional love, and the conditions involve becoming smaller and quieter. After a few false starts and wobbly moments, I think my sisters and I have all been exceptionally lucky in love. But we've made our own luck out of loving each other, and raising each other up. We hold each other in such esteem that we've set a very high watermark. Our romantic partners don't need to love our sisters, but they must love us as hard as our sisters do.

As women, I think we have a responsibility to each other. We might not constantly feel filled with love for each other. We might struggle to understand each other, and say things we might regret – and there's nothing like a hen party for bringing out our darkest sides. But it's very important that we build each other up, and don't diminish each other. When we feel positive and proud of who we are, we're more likely to find the love we deserve instead of seeking it out as a solution to low self-esteem.

When I was little, it was impressed upon me that I *had* to love my sisters – it wasn't something I could ever opt out of because biology had made my choice for me. Now I'm old enough to know that love is rarely a choice for anyone, but we can all decide how we love. We can be sparing and careful with our affection, and we can hold it back until we know what we might get in return. Or we can love volubly, bravely and hopefully, fuelled by the belief that we are worth loving. Dale told me that when he kissed me for the first time, by the barriers of London Bridge tube station, surrounded by drunk travellers and giggling schoolchildren, that I was 'worth being brave for'. His words made me better at loving everyone in my life. None of us are allocated that much time on Earth. I believe that in order to use it, we need to find the courage to take a leap to tell people that we love them, and to love ourselves enough to stay strong no matter what their answer is. If we're very lucky, our sisters and friends are the ones who show us how to find and even survive Big Love by showing us how to like who we really are.

CHAPTER EIGHTEEN
How to Be a
Grown-up Sister

I t's 3 October 2015. In just over half an hour, I will
hopefully be married to the man I love. My sisters and I
have arrived at the wedding venue much earlier than is
traditional. There was a mix up with Addison Lee, meaning
they travelled in air-conditioned comfort in a vast Mercedes,
while my dad and I rattled around in a slightly scratched
Ford Galaxy. It is unseasonably hot and sunny, the sort of
gorgeous English day you only get when you've made plans
that aren't contingent on the weather. I'm sweating heavily,
partly with nerves and partly because I'm wearing a heavy
veil. Grace is peering at the rivulets of sweat that are
dripping off my chin, leaving chalky tidemarks against my
fake tan, as though my face is made of sand and someone
has raked their fingers through it. 'Yes, I remember, it *does*
get hot in the veil.'

'Why are you only remembering this *now*? You've had
well over a year to tell me about the bloody veil.' Nerves are
making me bitchy, the acid in my stomach coating my
tongue. Maddy, who is dressed like Angelina Jolie at the 2013
Oscars, in a sexy black cocktail dress with slits up both sides,
decides to be our peacekeeper. Clearly, she is channelling

Angelina during her UN ambassador periods. 'We need to tell some jokes! What's the filthiest joke you know?'

Dotty thinks. 'What do you call a sex worker with her hand up her skirt?' She pauses. 'Self-employed.'

Beth adds: 'Man at a theatre turns to the woman next to him and says, "Can I smell your fanny?" She snaps, "ABSOLUTELY NOT!" So he replies, "Ah, then it must be my feet."'

'I've got one!' says Livvy. 'What's the difference between oral and anal sex? Oral sex will make your day, anal sex will make your whole week.'

We chuckle with different levels of heartiness. Grace's response seems a little lacklustre, so I assume she's heard it before. Then her eyes sparkle and she tips her head back and bellows, Brian Blessed with a bouquet. 'Oh! Oh oh HO!' she moans, wiping her cheek with the heel of her hand. 'I've just got it! Hole weak!'

This is my favourite tableau. My girls. Five beautiful, brilliant women, with dark hair, black dresses and a completely inconsistent taste in shoes, sharing the filthiest things they can think of. I'd spent a lifetime searching for my squad and I had to turn thirty to realise they were next to me all along. All I wanted in that moment was their presence. I didn't feel as though marriage meant leaving anyone behind. I felt closer to my sisters than I ever had, and I wanted them there to witness the biggest promise I would ever make.

Marriage is, I think, about celebrating many different kinds of love. It's an invitation to hope, and it forms a kind of alloy. You're combining romantic love with family love, layering it to last. At a wedding, when you declare your love for each other, while surrounded by family, you're saying, 'I love who you are, and who you have been – and I promise to love who you will become.' Dale knows that my sisters are the very best and worst of me. To varying degrees, we are all hypersensitive, quick-tempered, obsessive, overly anxious *Simpsons* addicts who eat too much cheese. But we're loving, loyal, imaginative, generous and good at seeing the funny side. I never feel more sure of who I am as an adult woman than I do when I'm with my sisters. And I never feel more fiercely, painfully engorged with hot pride than I do when I contemplate the women they have become.

Being a grown-up sister has been a challenge, and one that I have not always taken on with great grace. Bloody Grace. She's the sister who has helped me to grow up the most, largely because she assumed the mantle of adulthood with great alacrity while I was floundering about at the edge of my overdraft.

In the summer of 2011, I was sort of single, and utterly heartbroken. I was 'seeing' people – having semi-regular sex with various men that I didn't like very much, and pining after Voldemort, the ex-boyfriend who kept dumping me and then suggesting we get back together, seemingly because he enjoyed dumping me so much he wanted to do it as often as he could. I was twenty-six, and I'd just reached the point of my twenties where I was wondering whether all the 'fun' was really making me quite miserable.

Facebook seemed to suggest that there were two kinds of girls in the world. There were the Graces – elegant in deed if not always in name, whose lives were filled with weekly milestones: here a pay rise, there a company car, everywhere a proposal. The girls who kept Ted Baker in business, and batch-cooked a week's worth of packed lunches on a Sunday night.

Then, there were the Daisys – really, the oops-a-Daisys, because our lives were punctuated by mistakes and stumbles. Our bodies were marked with bruises of unknown provenance. Our phones were filled with numbers that had been stored as 'Dave's Friend from Koko', or 'Emma Glastonbury (Hat??)'. We never had any money, and when we did it got spent in the pub or Pret. We were warriors and adventurers with stories to tell, and we'd get drunk – OK, I'd get drunk and say, 'If I ever attempt to go to a garden centre, I want you to hit me over the head with a plant pot until my brain bursts out through my ears, and if necessary, you need to tell them to switch off the life support.' If I noisily spurned domesticity, surely no one could guess that all I ever wanted was to be in love with someone who loved me enough to spend Sunday in a garden centre with me.

I didn't know what I was doing – but I knew I was toxically jealous of Grace, and I doubted that she'd ever envied me. Grace had a special drawer where she kept *spare presents*, and had another drawer filled with ribbons and gift bags. I could barely remember to send a birthday card, and often had Kellogg's Krave for tea. Without milk. My bohemian shit was starting to stink.

Infuriatingly, Grace never once rubbed her choices in my face. Oddly, I longed for her to criticise me, in order to justify my feelings. It would have been much easier to resent her if we both agreed that I was a total disaster, instead of me just thinking it in secret. And then she had the audacity to get engaged.

At the time, I was on the train, trying to work out whether it was safe to use my bank card the night before pay day. I was also peering at a picture I'd been sent by a potential suitor. Every single girl at work had signed each other up to the same dating site, and the men in my inbox were marginally less exciting than the lawnmower section of the Argos catalogue. I was dating for something to do – anything to take the edge off the fact that I was bored and miserable at work, had been dumped three times in the last year, and had so much credit card debt that I'd taken to answering the phone in a generic foreign accent, just in case the Visa people were ringing to shout at me.

So when my little sister called to tell me her boyfriend had asked her to make him the happiest man in the world, I was staring at a photo of a stranger's erect penis. I remember frowning at the wrinkly, reddened flesh, at once strange and vaguely familiar, before the screen flashed and showed me a beautiful and beloved face. Wedding bells for Grace, bellends for Daisy. It was disconcerting. Grace's voice had a tremor in it. She wasn't calling to show off, but I think she understood that she was about to stir up some complicated feelings. Of course I said, 'That's the most wonderful news! I'm so happy for you!' Of course I smiled as hard as I could, in order to force my tone into a convincing version of 'happy'. And of course I burst into tears as soon as Grace hung up, just as the train pulled into Orpington and a man with a rucksack got on, saw my face and backed out of the carriage, stricken.

How could I handle this like an adult? More importantly, what if Grace had known the secret to happiness all along? I'd spent a lifetime trying to be cool, and wasted every second, making sad mix CDs for boys who would never fancy me, and buying weed from their friends, only for it to turn out to be PG Tips. Grace had it sussed from the second she slapped a tag protector on her first Beanie Baby, ignoring me as I made faces and chanted 'Nerd! NERD!'. She knew what was important to her and she wasn't going to be distracted by ideas about coolness. More importantly, a fiancé couldn't be stolen, or hidden under the bed, or dyed with contraband food colouring. I wanted her toys, and I couldn't take them. It wasn't that I nurtured a dormant passion for Ed, her husband-to-be, as charming as he was. I wanted her life.

I was familiar with this feeling, although it was rarely Grace who engendered it. Every Sunday night, I'd find myself in the throes of a sour Facebook trawl, actively looking for people with better lives than mine in order to make miserable comparisons. Looking back, I realise that I was extremely lonely. It was a bit like being an utterly shit superhero. By day, I'd do a terrible impression of a sorted single girl. Watch as she brags about her high-flying career, spending hours in the back boardroom waiting for a rescheduled phone interview with a boy band who might be (but probably aren't) the next One Direction! Behold as she orders a third bottle of rosé on a Wednesday, adding a last-minute request for a portion of chips and calling it dinner! Be amazed as she bravely buys a brand new backless bodycon dress on her credit card, just in case she bumps into her ex, even though she won't open the envelopes that tell her how much debt she's in! By night, I'd simply despair of ever finding anyone who might love me. All I wanted was someone who'd want to be with me forever.

Even though I knew, on an intellectual level, that the idea was nonsense, my dumb lizard brain really thought that everyone with a boyfriend had a perfect life. I'd go supermarket shopping with my friend Jonathan and his girlfriend Louise, and they'd have an argument over forgotten Bags for Life, or whose turn it was to put petrol in the car. Louise would get embarrassed and apologise for Jonathan – who was almost always the one being an unreasonable dick. A normal single person would silently congratulate themselves on their choices, perhaps buying a quarter-sized bottle of champagne to drink later, while they toasted the fact that they could do what they liked and weren't having sex with someone who liked to pick fights over plastic bags. Yet I envied Louise. I was a self-proclaimed, card-carrying feminist, but still, I thought that all I wanted in the world was to belong to someone.

At least my sisters and I belonged to each other. We were part of a gang, and made an unbreachable unit. But Grace was breaking up the group. She was happy, she was in love, and she was about to embark upon a new grown-up life without me. I never told her how I felt, and I simply assumed that I'd become an object of her pity. My position had been usurped, and her proposal meant my status changed overnight, from 'ambitious career girl' to 'spinster'. (Looking back, I now realise that if you're the sort of person who makes your sister's engagement all about you and your insecurities and inadequacies, you really can't be shocked that no one wants to marry you.)

At twenty-six, I knew I was two decades too old to be as jealous and upset as I felt. I was ashamed in about seventeen separate dimensions. Ashamed that no one had chosen me, ashamed that I envied my little sister, ashamed that I wanted to be loved and ashamed of having to lie, and pretend I was overjoyed. The shame was poisoning my blood, just as every peek at social media was adding to the toxins in my system. I was destroying any chance of joy in my own life by comparing myself to other people. Even though I wouldn't have been able to put this feeling into words at the time, much of my identity was built around the fact that at least Grace envied me. My little sisters had to think I was cool. In their eyes, I clearly wasn't the grown-up any more. I was nothing.

I'd like to be able to tell you that Grace's engagement forced me to fix myself. That I drew myself up to my full height, struck my breast and said, 'With God as my witness, I will stop wallowing in bullshit!' Honestly, I am still working at it. As usual, I was proved a fool by the future, and fell in love, very happily, within six months of declaring myself an unloveable loser. But finding someone to love you is relatively easy when you compare it to working out a healthy way to love and like yourself. I realised that I could only be a useful, helpful adult in the lives of my adult sisters if I worked on developing a private peace. Instead of striving for a heavily confected idea of perfection, and despairing when I fell some miles short of it, I needed to be able to look myself in the eye when I looked in the mirror. I had to find a way of seeing the parallel moles on my neck and shoulder, catching the whine in my voice when I asked for a favour, hearing the heaviness of my own ungainly footsteps and being able to think: 'This is me, and I am no better or worse, no more or less loveable than anyone else.'

Being a grown-up sister meant that being the 'big' sister could not matter so much. It meant that I had to stop thinking of my life in terms of order and disorder. Marriage was not like taking your GCSEs – the fabric of the universe would not be disturbed because Grace seemed to have got there early, and she hadn't made me late.

As a child, I'd been told that it was my job to create the standard, and set a good example. I felt as though the success of my sisters was contingent on my own, and if I'd not destroyed my mental equilibrium in order to get full marks in Maths, they would grow into lazy, barely literate women with life-threatening calculator dependencies. It took Grace's engagement to make me realise I'd got it all wrong. My only job as a big sister was to help them to find a balance between trying hard and being happy. I didn't want them to asphyxiate themselves while running to meet me and my achievements, in a place I'd only decided on because it seemed challenging and far away. I wanted them to go at their own pace, in a direction they had chosen. Sure, I felt as though my life was pathetic, and that it would be mysteriously less pathetic if I had a boyfriend. But I didn't want my sisters to feel that way, or that waiting to meet someone you truly loved and liked was less important than making sure you were married by the time you were thirty. I wanted them to feel confident and comfortable, to own their mistakes and to understand that you can't be alive without making any. However, as my twenties progressed, I was starting to feel as though my mistakes were piling up to the point of becoming unfixable. I hated myself for it.

It took me a long time to realise that I thought I wanted

advice, but I really longed for reassurance. Unbelievably, I knew what I was doing, and although I was making plenty of mistakes too, my life wouldn't be better if I had someone standing over my shoulder, pointing them out, as I texted Voldermort on the way back from a night out in Angel to say I was 'quite near' his flat in Barnet, which was seven miles away, or spent an entire working day reading Paris Hilton's Wikipedia entry. (Did you know that Paris tried to get off a drugs charge by saying the cocaine she had been accused of carrying was in a bag from 'a high-street brand', implying that if she were to use drugs, she wouldn't deign to keep them in anything less than a Prada purse? I love her so much.)

Anyway, like Paris Hilton, I kept making bad decisions – and unlike Paris, I didn't know why. Every seemingly stupid thing she did was a smart move, made with the intention of getting her picture in the papers and selling more perfume. Yet doing bad things on purpose, knowing they make you sad, is fractionally more stupid than showering with your jeans on.

Beth once suggested that I sort my life out by moving to Russia, where I could live in a boarding house for about nine pounds a year, and write a 'proper' book, instead of embarrassing us both by attempting to make a living out of interviewing N-Dubz. I realised that the biggest difference between us wasn't that she was an intellectual, and I fannied about with minor pop stars, but that we had opposite fight-or-flight responses. When she was unhappy, her instinct was to run far away. Mine wasn't to fight exactly, but to remain frozen to the spot, blinking and shaking. I needed a little bit of flight in my life, or at least, to mentally get far enough away from the stupid thing to understand the stupid thing. Distance brought perspective, which I needed in order to apply more compassion to my own life. As long as you've not purposefully burned your own house down, what you've done is almost never as damaging as the way you punish yourself for it afterwards.

I decided that I needed to work out how to spend time by myself, thinking happy thoughts instead of going on Facebook-sponsored descents into despair. This sounded grim. Usually, Sunday was the day I spent by myself, and it was the worst day of the week. I'd lie underneath my duvet, hungover and hollow-boned with paranoia, hating myself for my failure to go out and exercise, but also irrationally frightened of the shouty boys with bikes who hung out in the car park of the flat. I'd barely dress, not showering because I longed for a bath, and I didn't have one. I'd read the Sunday papers on my phone and feel the corrosive acid of envy rising in my blood, because I'd have given my arms and legs to write for the Sunday papers, but I didn't know where to begin. I wouldn't talk to anyone because I'd be too embarrassed and ashamed to explain that I was unhappy. Dad would ring, usually in the middle of the afternoon, and I'd massage the facts of the weekend into downright lies. 'Dinner with friends' was code for 'I went out after work, managed to lose everyone around Dean Street and was very sick in a hedge in Soho Square'. 'Going for a walk later' meant 'I am going across the road to buy own-brand Frazzles from Tesco Metro. I plan to eat these while watching *Sex and the City* on an illegal streaming site, and crying.'

Whenever I spoke to my family, I managed to make my

London life sound healthy, even borderline bucolic. 'You practically live in that park!' said Dad, after hearing about one of my imaginary runs. Financially, it wasn't far from the truth – I was only ever half a paycheque away from moving to the park. I put myself under so much pressure to be perfect that I couldn't bring myself to tell anyone that I was falling apart. Not even my sisters. I wanted to protect them from my messy life, and I needed to think that they might still look up to me. I was too proud to ask for help.

My Sunday routine needed some serious work, but I thought the day was too tainted for my initial attempts at self-improvement. I decided to try staying at home on Friday nights instead – or rather, to let go of my Friday night prejudice and accept that a good night in was better than a bad night out. I used to think that Friday could redeem the week. If I went berserk on a Friday, it proved my job was stressful and significant enough to warrant letting off some serious steam. A big night on Friday proved I was good at living for the moment, and it took the pressure off the rest of the weekend. The night might take me somewhere magical. Perhaps I'd meet the person who I'd be spending my Saturdays and Sundays with! Admittedly, it was unlikely that I'd meet them at Infernos on Clapham High Street.

However, Friday nights rarely lived up to the thrill their name conjured. Even now, I need reminding that when I picture my perfect Friday night, I'm not imagining a typical evening at all, I'm just thinking about Grace Kelly's engagement party in *High Society*. If I want to recreate a true Friday night experience, I just need to clamp my lips over a mouthful of sour, warm wine, the sort that tastes as though it's been mixed with the powdered food that comes in supermarket flower bouquets, and ride around Zone 3 on the top deck of a night bus for two hours. The buses were bad. The wine was bad. The mounting debt, the despair, the drugs, the ruined shoes were all very bad indeed. But the worst thing I did, the activity that tore at my outlines and started to erode my human core, was running after boys. It didn't matter that I kissed them, or sometimes slept with them. The problem was that I believed that getting attention from a stranger would validate me, and fix everything that was wrong with me. I didn't think I was worthy of a lifetime of love from anyone, but I could make myself loved for one night only. I was, I think, addicted to the Friday Night Boys. I don't know how many there were, and I can't remember their names – although I suspect about 40 per cent of them were probably called Jamie.

I was a hypocrite. I wanted my little sisters to be loved for themselves, and more importantly to love themselves, yet I was temporarily giving my heart away indiscriminately to men who both bragged about their bonuses and thought it was OK to wear flip-flops to the pub in February. It was time to take action. I decided that I'd go out on a Friday if it was someone's birthday, or if I was genuinely excited about the night ahead and I wanted nothing but straightforward fun with friends. If I was going out because I was sad, or scared, or simply wanted to get so drunk that I didn't have to think my own thoughts any more, I would stay in, and learn to like it.

Fridays became an occasion. For the price of a glass of unpleasant wine in central London, I could buy myself a miniature bottle of M&S vintage champagne. In a tiny, barely communal kitchen, on cheap electric oven rings, I learned how to cook expensive steak, rubbing oil and diced garlic all over it until the tips of my fingers shone, and waiting, no matter how hungry I was, for the pan to become so hot that it would gasp and rasp from the second the meat touched it. There was no dining table, and there were no friendly housemates, so I'd close my door and eat alone on my bed, candles lit and flickering along the windowsill, the faintly funereal scent of the lillies I'd bought myself filling the room and meeting the evening air. It was a wake, of sorts. I was mourning the girl I hadn't become: the responsible, settled, sorted girl I grew up believing I'd be. In trying to measure up to an imaginary fantasy, I'd forgotten how to exist. I needed to honour her memory in order to move. I'd been allowing myself to be shamed by a ghost.

Like most children, my sisters and I all believed that becoming a grown-up was a permanent state we'd all reach at a fixed point in time, as long as we kept finishing our homework and cleaning our teeth, and stopped running up three-figure phone bills on MSN Messenger. Up to a point, I believed it was my job to become a grown-up as quickly as possible, so I could pass the information on. As a child, I could imagine us all with houses, husbands and babies, although my imagination wasn't good enough to think of many specific characteristics for the babies or the husbands, who I pictured like Lego men, with vague variations in their rigid hypothetical haircuts. When we were all grown-ups, I thought, we'd never feel sad or scared any more. We'd be able to answer all of our own questions. Shamefully it didn't occur to me that husbands and wives, boyfriends and girlfriends could come and go, that babies might not turn up, and that being a mum didn't make you omnipotent. For a long time, I'd tried to be a grown-up for the sake of my sisters, without knowing what a grown-up was – a little bit like when Joey from *Friends* dressed up as his idea of a vicar, in shin pads and a hockey mask.

I spent so much of my twenties feeling lost, and looking for a grown-up. I sought out advice, mostly from the internet, and the advice was obvious and terrible. 'Why not get a job that pays more money?' 'Find a boyfriend who is sexy and adventurous, but invests conservatively with a stocks and shares pension!' 'Quick, there's not much time left – don't forget to put that spare £10,000 you have in an ISA before the end of the tax year!' Or my personal favourite: 'Spend your Sunday dehydrating berries, and stock up on Christmas presents! It's much more original than a scented candle – you can be sure that no one else will be giving your loved ones the gift of a jar filled with dried berries!' Some parts of the internet sound like a guide to adulthood that has been written by a child who stayed home from school with a temperature and watched the second half of *This Morning*, entranced.

Tiny champagne by tiny champagne, I taught myself to say, 'It's OK.' It's OK to be on your own. It's OK to be still. It's OK to be unsure of who you are, as long as you're up for finding out. It's absolutely OK to be twenty-six, or sixty-six, or 106, and eating steak by yourself in bed. Or in someone else's bed, as long as you're there out of joyful enthusiasm, and not because you're lonely or bored.

The hardest and most important part of being a

grown-up sister lies in acknowledging and accepting the fact that your sisters don't need to follow your path any more. They must live their own lives, and you're not allowed to look to them and expect their decisions to validate your choices. All you can do is be kind, and be generous about sharing what you did, and what you really learned, rather than giving unsolicited advice that is based on what you would have done with the benefit of hindsight.

CHAPTER NINETEEN
Death and the Maidens

I travel badly. When I'm subjected to forward motion for more than twenty minutes, a sort of stickiness descends. It's as if my body is digesting itself, and I become a composition of stale sweat, dead breath, cheap coffee and knotted hair. For years, I've been developing tricks to disguise my horrible, decomposing humanity, but nothing works. My sunglasses – modelled by Joan Didion herself in a billion-dollar hipster-friendly ad campaign – become smeared and grey. My handbag, which, pathetically, has become my sole totem of envied, responsible adulthood even though there is absolutely nothing admirable or responsible about carrying your phone around in something that costs the same as a month's rent on a Zone 2 studio flat – attracts a layer of dehydrated croissant crumbs, even when I haven't eaten a croissant that day. Every single layer of fake tan that I have ever applied in my life combusts, and I start to smell like a regurgitated rusk.

So when I got back from a few days in Spain with my friend Holly, I was dreaming about showering before I'd got through the passport barriers. I kept picturing my return home. I'd burst through the front door, throw my bags on a chair, shove my wheelie case aside as thought I was auditioning for *Airport: The Musical*, cuddle my husband while apologising for smelling like an unrinsed bin and then stand under the shower for a good twenty minutes. Maybe I'd get the Cif out if the Original Source was insufficiently lemon fresh. But the plan was interrupted. I got as far as the cuddle when my husband said, 'You're not to worry.' A kindly meant, four-word lie that stands in for the triple threat of: 'Be very afraid.'

'He's fine now.'

Who? Who is fine now? How could they be fine when something had obviously happened to them between now and me leaving the country, seventy-two hours ago?

'Your dad had a cardiac incident.'

My slow, stupid brain took minutes to unpick it. Cardiac was heart. An incident was what happened when local youths spray-painted 'SEX SHOP OPENING HERE' over the old newsagent shutters in the shopping precinct. An incident was when the Bishop of Southwark got drunk and broke into that man's car. My dad, the Bishop of Southwark, incident . . .

'Dad . . . had a heart attack?'

'Your mum told me not to tell you until you got back, because she knew you'd want to come home.'

'YES I'd want to bloody come bloody home! Mum!'

'But honestly, he is OK, he's had people with him, he's been to hospital, he's had a stent fitted.'

Dale explained to his stinky wife that his father-in-law had been feeling funny and had happened to go into work for a meeting with a colleague who'd had a heart attack a few months ago. The colleague recognised the warning signs, and managed to call Dad an ambulance, so he was attended by paramedics more or less as it happened. He had been lucky. He had been really, really lucky.

We are really, really lucky. My family are healthy. Not in a muesli and marathons sense, but in that I have spent very, very little of my life in hospital. I can count the occasions on one hand. I am the only one of the six Buchanan children that has ever broken a bone. But you don't appreciate what luck – what lottery-winning, four-leaf-clover-finding, crazy, against all odds luck that is until you're presented with the prospect of a loved one's mortality. Life is unavoidably fatal, and even though I sang 'in dying we are born to eternal life' every single week for eighteen years, I didn't think about what it meant until I realised that there had been maybe twenty minutes between eternity and Dad. It was time to make a pilgrimage.

I remember panicking at Waterloo, wondering whether it was safe to assume that Dad already had the newest Stephen King hardback, and if Kiehl's Face Fuel was a suitable gift for the man who had nearly lost everything. In Marks and Spencers, I picked up a bottle of champagne, to celebrate Dad's recovery, put it down, and then picked it up again, while trying to open my bag and find my phone with two spare fingers to Google whether good claret wasn't the better option for heart health. Dad was – *is* – a shopper, a man of great, grand generosity, and I have inherited his tendency to throw money about. I'm not sure whether his extravagance is noticeable because of Mum's frugality, or whether her financial anxieties and drive to save exacerbated his spendy sensibility, but shopping is his love language. I didn't know how to say, out loud, 'I am a grown-up and I have learned how to be brave for you,' so I hoped that a £30 pot of moisturiser would do the job.

I came home, not for Dad but for me. I felt very, very small, and I needed to be near the people that made me feel safe. On the train, a memory floated up unbidden: me at three years old, climbing on my father, a brave little girl seeking victory against a benevolent monster. I wielded imaginary swords and hurled jagged lightning bolts made of air, before collapsing into giggles and saying, ' I'm glad people don't really die!' At the time, I'd seen death referred to on TV, and assumed it was simply a convenient plot device, like being able to sprout wings on demand. I was small enough to take care of, then. I hadn't become big by default, the order of the family and the order of life forcing me to relinquish my vulnerability and become a caretaker.

The trouble with being a big sister is that you never really feel safe. It's your job to make the world safer for other people. In the games you play, you're always the big bad wolf, the wizened old crone, the person who has seen horror and absorbed it, so that the smaller players might stay little for longer. I was thirty-one years old, and I wanted to hurl myself into my father's arms and say, 'I'm so glad you're going to live forever!' when the point of my journey was that he *wasn't*. I wanted to be with my dad, but I needed to be with my babies, the little girls I had been big for, for my whole life, and soak up their pain. It was a test of strength, of durability, and I'd never felt more breakable.

Another memory was aroused. During my most awkward years, when puberty was at its most apparent and painful, but I still wasn't a proper teenager, we'd go on an annual family trip to a theme park called American Adventure World. It was in Derbyshire, about an hour's drive away from Dad's parents, and I think it acted as an overspill attraction for Alton Towers, in the next county over. (A Wikipedia deep dive reveals it opened in 1987, a time when the concept of America seemed more iconic and compelling than the moon. At one point in the early nineties, my sisters and I saw a programme about people coming out of comas and speaking in completely different accents. We'd take turns to stand on the sofa and throw ourselves to the ground, hoping to knock ourselves out and wake up American.) During my pubescent identity crisis, a trip to American Adventure World was a soul balm only marginally less soothing than a trip to America itself.

In the summer of 1995, American Adventure World had an exciting new attraction, a rollercoaster with *two* loops, right next to each other. I'd have a fight with Beth afterwards, because I claimed to be the only sister to have successfully looped the loop, and she'd say, 'You LIE! You did not loop *the* loop, you just looped and then did another loop. The only thing you looped was yourself!' Being able to say that I looped the loop was much more important than the sensation of looping. I did not want to go on the ride because I loved giddy, white-knuckle thrills. I thought the g-force would rip my nerdy exoskeleton from my body, and that there might be a cool girl underneath. I wanted to shed fat, bookish, precocious Daisy, the girl who would get the shit kicked out of her in the playground, then dust herself down and say, meaninglessly, 'You know, sarcasm is the lowest form of wit!' Also, I'd assumed that because it was a cool, manly, daredevil thing to do, that Dad would be keen. I longed to share something with him that excluded my other sisters. I wanted to cultivate a loveable quirk that could make him truly proud of me. I imagined him describing me to his colleagues at work. At the time, I assumed that if they were asked about me, my parents would say, 'Our eldest is quite chubby, she collects creepy Victorian repro china dolls and knows every single word to every song in *Evita*.' But this would make me 'Daredevil Daisy' instead.

The theme of the rollercoaster was Wolf from *Gladiators*, and I was grandiose and delusional enough to stand in the queue, my plump, sweaty hand in Dad's warm, dry one, and say, 'Maybe, one day, we'll come back here and they'll name a rollercoaster after me!' Dad would have been well within his rights to laugh heartily, or even to gently point out the athletic disparity between the professional foam pugil wielders and me. But he smiled and said, 'That would be nice!' I suspect that 60 per cent of this statement was born of kindness, and the other 40 per cent from petrified distraction.

I now know that Dad did not want to go on the rollercoaster. He had absolutely no desire to loop anything and would have been much happier watching from a bench while my sisters threw rapidly melting ice cream all over his trousers. But he was brave for me. So brave that I didn't know how much he had hated every single second of the Iron Wolf until 2007, when we heard that American Adventure World was closing down. Together, we remembered the problematic cowboys and Indians theme, the fetid, marshy smell that lingered in the family car for months after we'd all been on the Nightmare Niagara log flume, and an octopus-shaped ride, mischristened by Livvy as the Terrible Testicles. 'What was that awful thing you made me go on, with the two loops?' asked Dad. 'I've never been so frightened in my life. The only thing that stopped me from being sick was that I was very nervous about where the sick might end up, when we were in the air.'

No one is really, truly tough or brave. They are only ever pretending, either because there is something they don't love about themselves, or because it's their way of showing how much they love someone else.

I didn't know how Dad could survive the loops and be broken and battered by something as boring and inevitable as ageing. I didn't know why I thought that a rollercoaster, something I experienced entirely passively, could make me cooler and stronger when the knowledge of Dad's fragility and humanity had knocked the breath from my body.

Still, I was surprised to see that Dad made such a stately invalid. Every year, he becomes slightly more like Emma Woodhouse's father, generous but indulged, static but crackling, constantly watching, sensing, noticing, and reading the runes of his body with the focus of a genteel clairvoyant. 'There's a slight ache at the back of my throat, and my left arm is a little hotter than my right. *What does it mean?* he'll ask Mum, who might conjure something out of turmeric and Vicks VapoRub, or might mischievously say, 'Ah, that sounds like Gilbert's Syndrome. You'll be lucky to see out the month. Tell me, has the hot arm started to go green yet? That means it's about to drop off.'

Strangely, I think Dad was bolstered by the fuss. His hypochondriac tendencies had become valetudinarian, and his

keen interest in his own health and wellbeing had been
validated. He submitted to the attention with great grace, and
no little relish, while we all did some very human faffing. Do
you and your family ever want to sit down together to
contemplate the enormity of a tragedy that never was? No!
You want to saw your way through an unsliced farmhouse
loaf and compose ninety-six square ham and pickle
sandwiches, because wrist ache is slightly more bearable than
heartache. I'd imagined that my sisters and I would be lying
on the floor, weeping, as though we were in the throes of a
throwback Menstruation Special (absolutely *not* what Dad
would have wanted) but we were all being eerily adult. We
were being brave for each other.

I will all really die. We will have to come together and
try to understand how to feel when we don't strike out with a
near miss. I make the mistake of trying to protect myself
from future pain by bringing the idea of it into the present,
and I wonder how we'll manage. Together, my sisters and I
have lost four grandparents: John, Francis, Kath and then
Peggy. We watched our parents, and wondered how to be
brave for them, what you can possibly say to someone who
has lost such a big and complicated love.

I know that it helps to make space for their words,
instead of overwhelming them with yours. I know that most
people have an instinctive urge to try to minimise their loss,
because they hate to see a loved one hurting, and they long to
take the pain away. Instead, you must give them the room to
be sad, let their sadness fill ballrooms and stadiums, show
them that it's OK to want the world to stop, and you will
slam the brakes on for them, as hard as you can, and that

their loss needn't make sense – the rest of reality can be warped in order to make a new context for it.

Mum has a deep, profound faith, and she once told me that she thinks about death all the time. I can't think about my bank balance without yelping, and the fact that she is prepared to embrace the reality of mortality really does make her the bravest person I know. Dad does not talk about death and dying as Mum does. Like most normal people, he doesn't really talk about it at all. When I almost lost him I gleaned the smallest insight into what his grief must have felt like when his parents died. Worrying about whether I was good enough, thinking about the ways in which I must have disappointed him, wondering when I should have spoken and when I should have stayed silent.

Love must be loud. I'm often afraid to speak because I'm so nervous that my words won't do justice to the nuance of my feelings, that I can't refine, revise and edit when I go live. I can't say what I mean or how I feel in case I get it wrong. Loving someone is an act of bravery and you can't do it quietly. But you can find strength in showing your love, in sharing your deepest fears, and telling someone that your love for them defies explanation, and that you have remembered every single time they were brave for you. And you can pay the bravery forward, at weddings and christenings and funerals, during thunderstorms and redundancies, and when queuing for rollercoasters.

I think this is the legacy of family. We protect each other instead of ourselves. We find a muscle we didn't know we had and stretch it taut. It prevents us from falling apart. Family is sandwiches and arguments and retaining obsessive petty details for decades, and farting in each other's faces, but it's all love. While I will never think I'm strong enough to look after myself, I have to be, because I must find the strength to look after my five best girls. And I don't need to be, because they'll all be looking out for me. It makes us tearful and tense and irrational, it means some stories are hidden forever, and others are revisited far too often, becoming less of an oral history and more of a fiction written by six of the most unreliable narrators in the world. The only thing we can agree on is that we all exist, and that lying, exaggeration and embellishment is probably justifiable if they make the jokes funnier.

But that's why I have the audacity to tell the tale on their behalf. I do not trust them to be honest about how very brave they can be.

CHAPTER TWENTY
My Advice for my Sisters

If a pair of shoes costs £800, and they have been reduced to £200, buying them doesn't 'save' £600. It means you've spent £200.

It's better to be a year or five late for your smear test or the dentist than it is to not go.

If you're having a heated argument with a friend about celebrities called Jeremy, and you can't see eye to eye, check that one of you isn't saying 'Clarkson' when you mean 'Paxman'.

When you're mucking about in Duty Free, *spray the perfume on the little card.* Not on you. This is for your sake, and the sake of whoever you're sitting next to on the plane.

Eat when you're hungry, stop when you're full. Don't feel obliged to clear your plate unless you definitely want to eat it. Throwing food away isn't ideal, but it's better than having indigestion.

If it's remotely possible, try not to get too hung up on the state of your upper arms. Some of the best and smartest women I know would probably be ruling the world as we speak, if they weren't expending quite so much mental energy on fretting over their arms.

Bullies, sadly, aren't rare, and you'll definitely encounter at least one in your life. Also, if you ask for help, someone will inevitably suggest that you 'just ignore them'. This is terrible advice! Bullying is hurtful and no one has the right to hurt you. It's OK to be sad and angry and vulnerable. It's OK to feel your pain. However, I wish I'd known that most bullies are in a lot of pain too. It's not your responsibility to help them, but you need to know the badness comes from them, not you. Most bullies have been bullied, and they've had nowhere for that pain to go. Let yourself be sad, and scared and hurt. If you're not getting anywhere when you ask for help with the bully, ask for help to handle your feelings. Remember that playground bullies are easy to identify but grown-up bullies can take us by surprise. If you practise your emotional core strength, and stay as true as you can to who you know you are, you can survive the baddest bully.

Exercise! I avoided exercise for years because I knew I'd never be the fastest, strongest or skinniest. I wish I'd known how good it feels, and that it's not about doing it well – it's about getting into your body and forcing your mind to forget that you care about doing things well. It's about falling in love with your arms and legs because you suddenly realise what they can *do*. The more you exercise, and the bolder and buzzier the endorphin rush becomes, the less you worry about looking stupid. And that's a superpower.

The world won't end if you try smoking, or drugs, or end up ditching your dinner behind some bins outside an establishment called Ziggy's. It's OK to have fun, and it's OK to do things you end up regretting as long as your life isn't defined by that regret. By all means party but pay attention to the way it makes you feel. If you don't like people when they're sober, they are not your people.

Be especially wary of white wine at lunchtime. It seems like a sweet little old lady, offering you an apple from under its shawl, but it's the wicked queen of drinks, and if you fall under its spell it will dump you in the woods and it doesn't care how you're getting home.

If someone introduces themselves to you as 'the kind of person who tells it like it is' or says 'I speak as I find and I don't pull any punches' – run, quite fast, in the other direction.

Never buy any 'classic' clothing if you try it on and it makes you feel a little bit heavy and low, as if you're compromising your secret, special self. Black trousers aren't a handy wardrobe essential if you can't look at them without thinking, 'Urghhh, my useful, practical trousers.' If a garment's USP is that you can spill coffee on it but the stain doesn't show up, leave it be.

Conversely, you would be surprised to learn just how much wear you can get out of a gold sequinned maxi skirt.

There is a very fine line between the amount of caffeine that makes you feel awake, alert and ready to face the challenges of the day, and the amount that makes you feel like bursting into tears and hiding under the bed. Respect the line. It's always better to feel sleepy and slow than to be frightened of your own heartbeat.

Regrets are inevitable, but try to make sure that you never regret not being kinder. Be as generous and compassionate as you can afford, and understand that your capabilities in this area will wax and wane. If you send flowers to people you love when the mood takes you, it's not a disaster if you occasionally forget to post their birthday cards.

Similarly, no one will stop speaking to you if you go to their dinner party and don't have a chance to pick up some wine on the way. You definitely don't need to bring two kinds of hummus either.

Heartbreak can be a bit like having a very bad cold, in that there are moments when it feels endless, and absolutely impossible to survive. You always get through it and recover. The hardest trick is to remember enough of what it's like in order to endure it better next time.

If you can make a roux, you can make lasagne, cheese sauce, creamed spinach and pasta bake. Fry garlic or onions in the butter before you add the flour, and whatever you make will be tastier. The most important thing is to hold your nerve when you're looking at your panful of milk and globs of flour, which seems to bear no relation at all to anything that anyone might want to eat. Keep stirring and everything will become smooth.

You can shave or wax if you want to, and it doesn't make you a tool of the patriarchy. Similarly, you're under no obligation to be smooth for anyone but you. However, hair removal is a little bit like beheading the Hydra. The second you've done your shins, you'll discover an odd thicket of pubes just behind your knee. Approach the management of your body hair with the knowledge that life is short, and has much more exciting and absorbing activities in it.

You will die before you've read all of the books you'd like to read. That is one of the greatest tragedies and most thrilling aspects of being a human. If you're a reader, you will constantly become kinder and wiser, and your life will always be filled with adventure. If you connect with the classics, that's great, but it's equally valid to fill your shelves with *Sweet Valley High* books.

When at the airport or on a long journey, always respect the wishes of the most anal, paranoid traveller in your party. Being overly relaxed doesn't have a calming effect on the other passenger; it just makes you a total arsehole. Let them set the pace, and you'll get Security out of the way and you can have a cup of tea or gin and tonic.

If you're going to be mean, be judicious with it. We all need to bitch, vent and complain, but don't make bitching the principal part of your personality. Watch out for people who are constantly cruel. Make a habit of pointing out the positive. If you realise that you and a friend only ever talk to slag off mutual acquaintances, stand back and get some distance. Gossip is like farting. Sometimes, it truly is better out than in, but you need to be extremely careful about when and where you do it, otherwise you'll make everything stinky and no one will want to stand close to you at parties.

Throw away laddered tights. You're not going to use them for a craft project. You're not going to need them to escape from your room, Rapunzel-style, if your house is under siege. If there is a nuclear winter, you'll be vaporised long before it gets cold enough to wear them under your jeans.

Aim to change your bedsheets once a week, but don't beat yourself up if you only manage it once a fortnight.

Be very careful about mentioning your fondness for a particular celebrity, animal or motif, unless you want your kindly, well-meaning friends and relations to fill your house with Elvis coasters and faux Route 66 road signs. This is why 85 per cent of the cushions in my house have lobsters on them.

You can avoid ironing most things by taking them into the bathroom with you when you're having a shower. However – and I can't stress this enough – do not take them into the shower itself.

No one ever really tells you how complex and complicated friendship is. It takes a lot of work, and sometimes the work just isn't worth it. Never feel as though you've failed because a friendship hasn't lasted forever. Never think that a friendship has ended permanently either. You will both change, and sometimes you'll find that after some time elapses you fit together much more comfortably than you did the first time you tried it.

Don't lend anyone a book if you know your heart will be broken if you don't get it back. For books you truly love, it might be worth investing in a 'lending' edition. (Every time I see a copy of *Valley of the Dolls* I buy one because I always end up giving them away.)

Remember, you can do anything and everything, but it's OK to do nothing. The only way that you can truly fulfil your potential is to make choices that make you happy. You can't serve yourself by following someone else's definition of success if it's going to make you miserable. Plenty of people aren't sure about their life choices, and they might make confusing comments about yours, simply because they're seeking to validate their own. Making a million pounds won't make you happy if you find yourself surrounded by people who tell you that you now need to make ten million. If enormous amounts of uncertainty make you miserable and keep you up at night, you probably don't really want to quit your safe, straightforward job to become a sculptor. Success isn't about being impressive – it's living in a way that you don't need to defend, that makes you feel as though your insides match your outsides.

Stop burning your tongue. You can wait another thirty seconds. If this is the only area in which you learn to exercise impulse control, you will have learned an extremely useful skill.

If someone invites you to play mini golf, don't immediately say no, but remember that it gets *quite* tedious around the eighth hole.

Try to make sure that social media doesn't become a room in your head, in which you're perpetually hovering in the doorway trying to work out what it was that you came in for. It's not a bad thing, but it's too powerful to use carelessly. You're juggling with the thoughts and feelings of almost everyone in the known world, and you're going to need gloves and goggles. Remember that everyone has an agenda, and you'll never know what it is. All you can do is keep yours positive, cheerful and mindful. Remember, if you're feeling low, social media is probably not the place that will make your bad mood better.

What will improve your mood is the YouTube video of Debbie Harry and Kermit the Frog singing 'Rainbow Connection'.

Checking your bank balance is always grim and depressing, but it's a super fun activity compared with lying in bed at 3 a.m. thinking horrifying thoughts about what your bank balance might be.

Look for ways to help, and work out ways of asking for help that feel comfortable. Both things are scary, and will make you feel vulnerable, and not everyone you approach will want to help or be helped. That's OK. When it goes right, you'll be part of one of the most joyous, powerful elements of the human experience.

Optimism is a wonderful thing – just not when you've got the shits. Don't assume it will probably just be all right and go away. Don't get a train to Cornwall if you think there is even a 5 per cent chance that you might fart and follow through. You're strong, powerful women who can get through anything, but being caught on a Virgin Pendolino loo with an overly responsive door, when you have your knickers around your ankles, can take *months* to recover from.

The Worst Things to Say to Sisters

(or the Worst Things Anyone Has Said to, or About Us)

Kate, the lady who worked at the local beauty salon and used to administer mine and Beth's teenage bikini waxes: It's funny, because you're so much fairer than your sister, but your hair down there is exactly the same. Really coarse and wiry.

A new neighbour: I've seen you all out and about. What's the name of the pretty one?

An ex-boyfriend, who should have been dumped immediately after he uttered these words: Have you ever thought about sharing vibrators?

My mum, during a family picnic, when Livvy drank three bottles of Orangina: Your sister has wet herself again. You're going to have to give her your trousers.

My boss, who made me recruit Beth to work on a till and started asking about Grace: So she's not *technically* legally old enough to work, but how tall is she?

An auntie, to Livvy, at Beth's wedding: Are you enjoying your sister's wedding? Does it make you think you want to get married some day? Some day soon? Have you thought about getting a move on, because me and your uncle have just booked to go on a cruise in 2019?

The Sisterhood

My first boyfriend's mum, who believed that the main function of sisterhood was grooming: Your hair's a real mess at the back. Why didn't you get one of your sisters to put some straighteners through it before you left the house?

My mum, before my twenty-first birthday party: I thought Grace could help me with the cake decorations, because she's artistic. Here, why don't you wash that bin out so we can use it as an ice bucket!

Everyone: So, your husband has four brothers! Why don't they marry your sisters?
(Answer: Because most of them are already married, because he's the youngest, I'm the eldest, and you can't pair a sixty-year-old with a 25-year-old because of a musical you watched once.)

More than one ex-boyfriend: Five sisters, eh? Did you ever . . . practise kissing on them?

Charlotte, a girl I used to go to lectures with: Are they all like you, or is there a clever one?

A lady in Balham who was being paid to give me a manicure, after requesting to see a photo of us all: I guess they got the faces and you got the boobs!

Various boys, primary school: Why is your sister so weird?

Various boys, secondary school: Why is your sister so much hotter than you?

Our old piano teacher: It's funny, because you've all got such long fingers – yet not one of you is any good at this.

CONCLUSION:
What is Sisterhood?

Sisterhood is a state, not a story, and it doesn't have the arc of a traditional romance. Our strength of feeling turns like the tide, switching between violence and serenity in the same day, sometimes in the same hour. Yet, this is a love story, and it has a happy ending.

I have come to love my sisters more and more, as they become less and less like me. Still, that love surges when I discover a surprising similarity. We live different lives in different cities and we still keep mimicking each other, without realising. I am shocked and dazzled by their personhood. We're no longer a basket of fractious puppies, a jumble of tails and paws. We are women, humans, individuals. We have different dreams. But the more we are apart, the more we grow together. Now that there is room for difference, there is room for love.

It's a sense of sisterhood that draws me to other women. Sometimes this is a response to something shared, and sometimes I find them compelling because of our differences. Because if two women spend enough time together, they will find in each other a twin and an alien. We share histories, hopes and bodies, we mirror each other to the point of claustrophobia. But we will be presented with the same opportunities and problems and make completely different choices from each other in a way that seems both thrilling and bewildering. Sisterhood is a hard thing to be a part of because it requires so much cognitive dissonance. We look the same, we talk the same, but we could not be more different.

There are infinite ways to be a woman, and not one of them is right. I try to hold this idea close to my heart when I think about one sister's decision to live within ten miles of the house she grew up in, when I worry she has professional dreams that can't survive within this geographical comfort zone. I try to remember it when I think of a cherished friend who continues to give her heart away to a man who does not look at her with love in his eyes. I force myself to consider it whenever I see a picture of Melania Trump. I would not make some of the choices these women have made. But no matter how intimate our relationships are, I can never presume to know them well enough to judge them.

All you can do is encourage the women you love to feel secure in their choices. That way, they won't feel the need to tell others how to live their lives either. This is the point at which sisterhood extends beyond the biological. Admittedly, we *know* another woman is a true sister, regardless of parentage, when the urge to control and question kicks in. 'Are you sure you don't want to get pregnant *immediately* just in case you regret not doing it in ten years?' 'Didn't you know that the label of your top is sticking out?' 'Are you really going to eat that sandwich after five o'clock?' I think this is the most unfiltered, compassionate part of the *id*. It means: 'I wouldn't do that, if I were you – and I'm telling you because I love you so much that I'm not sure where it is that I end and you begin. It's a selfish, simple love, and it's not helpful to either one of us, but it's love all the same.' I think the challenge for today's sister is to learn that loving someone is not the same as understanding them. If we work harder at the latter, we shall strengthen the former.

That's not to say that sisterhood isn't often a thrilling celebration of sameness. At the end of 2017, I was invited to an early screening of Greta Gerwig's film, *Lady Bird*. I sat in the middle of a five-person row, in the midst of a gang of adopted sisters. There was Lauren, the first person I thought about taking as soon as I discovered that I had two tickets. Fleur, a new but beloved friend I had bumped into at the screening; Fleur's friend, a woman I had enjoyed talking to on Twitter; and Sarah, another friend I'd not seen for months. At one point, when the protagonist is arguing with her mother, our row spontaneously reached out to clasp each other's hands, and burst into tears in unison. The auditorium was filled with three distinct sounds – the voice of Saoirse Ronan, the voice of Laurie Metcalf, and the sound of three hundred women weeping softly and without inhibition. Whenever I have felt alone (and there have been many moments), I remember that evening, sitting in a cinema full of sisters and acknowledging an emotion shared. Even though we weren't bonded by blood, we were completely connected by our reactions to what was happening on screen. You don't need to be a mother or a sister to know how it feels to long to be loved, or just to be seen. I believe that every woman watching saw some of her own vulnerability on screen in that moment, but was strengthened by the knowledge that everyone else in the room was sharing that feeling.

The Sisterhood

I am a sister. That means I belong to Beth, Grace, Livvy, Maddy and Dotty. Even though there have been times when I thought I hated them, periods when I've failed to understand them, and conversations when I have violently disagreed with them, I adore them with a love that's bigger than logic. That love is indelible, and it brings me confusion and clarity. Choosing to define myself as a sister also means that I have a duty of care to all women. I don't have to like them – women can be just as soul-sappingly tedious as men, *that's* equality for you – but it's important to me to live a life that looks outward, to raise other women up whenever I can and to ask questions about how we can make life better for each other. When Meghan Markle asks questions about period poverty, she is being sisterly. When Emma Watson acknowledges that her feminism has not been sufficiently intersectional, and that she needs to address the privilege of race, that's sisterly. When Jameela Jamil launches an Instagram account that invites women to share their achievements before judging their bodies, she is being a sister to all of us. Sisterhood is not sainthood. We can't always get it right, we'll make mistakes and fight and bite and tell on each other sometimes. But we can be kind and compassionate. We can show up. As my mother used to say, 'Sisters! Love each other!' It never stopped us arguing. But we do love each other, and we're always trying to work out the best way to show that love. If you want to be a sister to women, that's the only advice you need.

ACKNOWLEDGEMENTS

This book is, I hope, a thank you to E, G, O, M + D – for a lifetime of love and laughter. Thank you for your generosity and support – I will never thank you enough for letting me tell some of your stories and secrets. I hope I'm not too unreliable a narrator. Also, thank you to Mum and Dad – for my sisters, for a house full of music and jokes and words and silliness, and especially for all the ABBA. P&A – one day in the distant future, I hope you read this and realise just how much I love your Mums and Aunties.

Thank you to my agent Diana Beaumont, for her constant kindness, enthusiasm, good cheer and positivity. Thank you to everyone at Headline, for making this book happen, and especially my wonderful editor Grace Paul.

Love and thanks to my early readers and cheerleaders, especially the JCBC (or Cleavage Rhombus, at the time of writing) and my South London Lovers – you have been my colleagues and companions during the writing of this book, and it's because of you all that I didn't throw my laptop out of the window. Lucy V, Dolly, Julia, Marina – I love you, thank you for making me laugh, being kind and being in my corner.

A special thank you to Mickey, Janie, Rory, Charlie – and Angela, Rowan, Julie, the Kates, Claire, Mark, Cally, Paul and

Richard, and everyone I've written with at the magical Chez Castillon. I love being part of your gang.

Huge, huge thanks to every single person who read *How To Be A Grown Up*, or listened to *You're Booked* – I honestly could not do this without your support, and every single reader and listener I have spoken to has made me feel so loved and lucky. I can't thank you enough. Especial thanks to all of our guests.

Much love and thanks to all of my *Pool* pals, especially the excellent Sam B, Zoe, Amy, Cate – and to all of the editors and writers who have been such a pleasure to work with. It's because of you that I love my job so much.

Big, big love and thanks to Lauren Bravo. In the words of Paris Hilton, almost, Lauren knows what she did. I couldn't write without you. Or dress, or feed myself, or leave the house.

Finally, this is for my darling husband Dale. Every single thing I write happens because I'm trying to make you laugh. You make my life so joyous and love filled. I hope you know that this book is a love letter for family – you are my family, and this makes me profoundly happy.